PASS
Cambridge
BEC Higher

Second Edition

Teacher's Book

Louise Pile and Catrin Lloyd-Jones *with* Sarah Curtis

NATIONAL GEOGRAPHIC LEARNING | CENGAGE Learning

Australia • Brazil • Japan • Korea • Mexico • Singapore • Spain • United Kingdom • United States

**Pass Cambridge BEC Higher Teacher's Book
Second Edition**
Louise Pile and Catrin Lloyd-Jones *with*
Sarah Curtis

Publisher: Jason Mann

Senior Commissioning Editor: John Waterman

Editorial Project Manager: Karen White

Development Editor: Sarah Curtis

Marketing and Communications Manager:
  Michelle Cresswell

Content Project Editor: Denise Power

Production Controller: Tom Relf

Head of Manufacturing and Production:
  Alissa McWhinnie

Cover Design: Maria Papageorgiou

Compositor: MPS Limited, a Macmillan Company

Audio produced by the Soundhouse Studio, London

ISBN: 978-1-133-31752-4

National Geographic Learning
Cheriton House, North Way, Andover, Hampshire, SP10 5BE, United Kingdom

Cengage Learning is a leading provider of customised learning solutions with office locations around the globe, including Singapore, the United Kingdom, Australia, Mexico, Brazil and Japan. Locate our local office at: **international.cengage.com/region**

Cengage Learning products are represented in Canada by Nelson Education Ltd.

Visit National Geographic Learning online at **ngl.cengage.com**

Visit our corporate website at **www.cengage.com**

We are grateful to the following for permission to reproduce copyright material:

IKEA for information and audio interview about IKEA on page 98. Reproduced with permission.

In some instances we have been unable to trace the owners of copyright material and we would appreciate any information that would enable us to do so.

Printed in China by RR Donnelley
3 4 5 6 7 8 9 10 – 17 16 15 14 13

Teacher's Book Contents

Student's Book Contents — Language — Exam Skills

	Language	Exam Skills

The Cambridge BEC examination

The Cambridge Business English Certificate (BEC) is an international exam designed to assess candidates' ability to use English in an international business environment. Paper-based exams are offered up to seven times a year and computer-based exams are offered more frequently. Teachers are advised to check with their local centres for exact dates. For further information see the Cambridge ESOL website.

Cambridge BEC is available at three levels, linked to the levels of traditional Cambridge examinations. The exams are linked to the Common European Framework of Reference for Languages: Learning, teaching, assessment, published in 2001 by the Council of Europe. BEC Preliminary is at B1 level, BEC Vantage is at B2 level and BEC Higher is at C1 level.

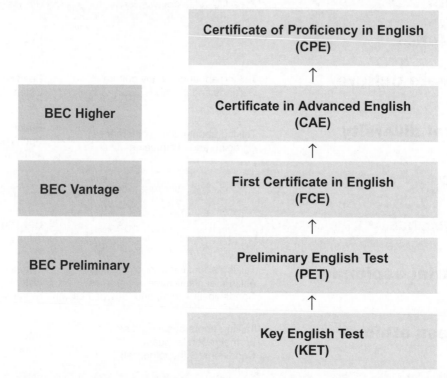

Cambridge BEC Higher is equivalent to CAE level. It is a practical examination that focuses on English in business-related situations. There is little focus on grammar in the examination and the major emphasis is on the use of language skills: reading, writing, listening and speaking. Each paper counts as 25% of the total mark. All candidates receive a grade (Pass grades A, B, C or Fail grades D, E) and a chart showing their strengths and weaknesses. Successful candidates also receive a certificate with their overall grade.

Pass Cambridge BEC Higher

Student Book

The Student Book contains:
- **Contents:** A two-page overview of the language and skills practised in the book.
- **Introduction:** An introductory unit which provides information about the examination and the preparation course.
- **Core units:** Eight double units which cover a wide range of business-related topics.
- **Self-study:** A section following every double unit to provide consolidation of the language of the units and some examination-related tasks. Each Self-study unit also contains a focus on a particular grammatical area.
- **Exam practice:** A section following Self-study which provides practice in all parts of the examination, supplementing the examination practice in the core units and Self-study.
- **Exam focus:** A section which prepares students directly for the Reading, Listening, Writing and Speaking Tests. This section provides additional information about the different aspects of the exam as well as tips for preparing and taking it. It also includes Assessment Sheets for the Speaking and Writing Tests.
- **Audioscripts:** The content of the two Audio CDs.
- **Answer key:** Answers to Self-study and Exam practice.

Workbook with Answer key

The workbook provides a language-focused supplement to the Student's Book:
- **Essential revision:** Follows the topics and language syllabus of the Student's Book.
- **Grammar and Vocabulary:** Each four-page unit is split into grammar and vocabulary sections.
- **Language Review:** two review units consisting of 100 grammar questions and 50 multiple-choice vocabulary questions based on the previous four units.

Self-Study Practice Tests with audio CD and Answer key

The Self-Study Practice Tests contain:
- **Three complete practice tests:** Reading, Writing, Listening and Speaking tests with sample Cambridge ESOL answer sheets.
- **Focus on key grammar, words and phrases:** To enable students to successfully approach every task in the examination.
- **Full Audioscripts:** For each listening test.

Audio CDs

There are two Audio CDs:
- **Class CD:** The listening material for the core units (approximately sixty minutes).
- **Exam focus CD:** There are two complete Listening Tests on the audio CD. The audio CD also contains Exam focus: Speaking. This contains mock interviews and also seven model answers for the one-minute talks. The total audio CD lasts approximately eighty minutes.

Teacher's Book

The Teacher's Book consists of the following material:
- Full teacher's notes with answers to all exercises. Answers are bolded in some audioscripts for the teacher's quick reference.
- Expanded Introduction.
- Photocopiable cards to accompany core exercises in Units 2a and 3a, alternative activities in Units 6b, 7a and 8b and the Exam focus: Speaking section.

Language development in *Pass Cambridge BEC Higher*

- ## Reading

  The book contains extensive reading practice, using authentic, semi-authentic and examination-style texts representing a variety of genres.

  Students should be encouraged to read very carefully when answering examination questions; sometimes the most obvious answer on the first reading is not correct.

- ## Writing

  The Writing Test is potentially difficult for students. Even if their spoken English is of a high level, they may lack experience in writing English; they will therefore need to learn and practise the necessary skills in order to perform well in this test. Students need to recognise the genre required in each question in the Writing Test; they therefore need to develop familiarity with the features of descriptions of graphs, formal proposals, pieces of business correspondence and short reports. The test is also challenging due to the specific nature of the instructions and the fact that task fulfilment is of key importance. The book contains systematic work on writing skills in the core units and in **Exam focus: Writing**. Further writing practice is provided throughout the core units, **Self-study** and **Exam practice**.

- ## Listening

  The book includes a wide variety of listening material throughout the core units. The **Audioscripts** to the two audio CDs can be found at the back of the Student Book and the Teacher's Book. In the Student Book, the audioscripts from the **Exam focus** audio CD are shown in blue.

  > For both reading and listening, the emphasis in the examination is on looking for specific information rather than understanding gist. Although teachers' priority is to train their students in examination skills, it is also useful if teachers include additional activities to develop general reading and listening skills when time permits.

- ## Speaking

  Students may be nervous about the Speaking Test and will need to be fully prepared for it. The **Exam focus** section outlines the format of the Speaking Test and gives strategies to help students perform well in all three parts. The section also includes materials for students to practise part of a mock Speaking Test. Furthermore, all core units provide fluency practice and opportunities for students to work together in pairs and groups. Speaking test preparation packs are available from Cambridge ESOL. Students can watch a complete speaking exam to get an idea of how the exam works and what will be expected of them.

• Vocabulary

Although vocabulary is tested explicitly only in Reading Test Part Four, it is very important throughout the examination. Therefore, vocabulary is systematically recycled in the **Self-study** section after each double unit. There is also extra vocabulary practice in the workbook.

• Grammar

The book assumes a certain level of grammatical knowledge. However, a grammatical point is covered in most units and grammar is systematically reviewed in the **Self-study** sections following each double unit. The **Contents** pages provide an overview of these grammar points. Nevertheless, the grammar review is brief and teachers may need to supplement the material. At the end of the teacher's notes for each unit, some brief notes on key language are provided for teacher support; these may also need to be supplemented with other reference material. There is some grammar practice in the workbook.

• Optional tasks

At the end of most units there is an **Optional task** for students to do between lessons, the main aim of which is to link the lesson with the outside world. This task may require students to write a report or prepare a presentation, providing an opportunity for further language skills practice.

Many of these tasks involve students accessing the internet. If students do not have internet access, other relevant materials can be recommended (e.g. newspapers, company reports, brochures). Students should be aware that, as with any authentic materials, some information may have become dated since publication.

Preparing students for Cambridge BEC Higher

What is available?

The following are available:

- *Pass Cambridge BEC Higher*

- *BEC Handbook for Teachers* (which includes sample papers and a CD). This can be ordered from Cambridge ESOL or downloaded from the website.

- You can also buy past BEC Higher Papers directly from Cambridge ESOL. In addition there are Speaking Test Preparation Packs, Exam reports and other Teaching resources (classroom activities) available to download from their website.

- Teachers who contact Cambridge ESOL can often get free training sessions on the exams. If a group requests this, Cambridge ESOL tries to find a presenter to send them and pays the presenter. Contact Cambridge ESOL for more information.

Examination preparation in *Pass Cambridge BEC Higher*

- **Introduction**

  The **Introduction** presents the content of the examination.

- **Core units and Self-study**

  Every unit contains at least one examination-style exercise. There is also some examination practice in **Self-study**, particularly for **Writing Test Part One** and **Reading Test Part Four**, **Part Five** and **Part Six**.

- **Exam practice**

  Each double unit is followed by at least two pages of **Exam practice** which supplement the examination practice in the core units and **Self-study**. Complete Listening Tests follow Unit 4 and Unit 8. By the end of the book, students will have systematically practised every part of the examination.

- **Exam focus**

  Exam focus is in one section at the centre of the book. This section provides information about the Reading, Listening, Writing and Speaking Tests and trains students directly in techniques for successful examination performance. It can be used whenever the need arises for a focus on a specific part of the examination. This section also contains Assessment Sheets for the Writing and Speaking Tests. Students need to be trained to use these sheets for self and peer assessment from the start of the course. (See the **How to succeed** sections of **Exam focus: Writing** and **Speaking** for further information on introducing students to the Assessment Sheets.)

Specific examination exercises in *Pass Cambridge BEC Higher*

Activities which are specifically related to the Speaking Test are outlined below. Exercises which are related to the Reading, Writing and Listening Tests are indicated in the grid opposite; these exercises may be found in the core units themselves or in **Self-study** or **Exam practice**.

In general, **Self-study** exercises carefully recycle vocabulary; however, the vocabulary in **Exam practice** exercises is not restricted to that of the double unit it follows. Therefore, should teachers wish to practise a specific examination question, they can choose from any **Exam practice** in the book.

Activities related to the Speaking Test

Exam focus: Speaking prepares students for all parts of the Speaking Test. Students hear poor and good versions of Part Two and Part Three of a mock Speaking Test. They also have the opportunity to practise the Speaking Test themselves.

In addition, specific practice for Part Two and Part Three of the Speaking Test can be found in the following units:

Part Two **(Short talk)**	**Units 3b, 5b, 7b** and **8a** involve students giving a one-minute talk. Model answers for the one-minute talks are provided on the **Exam focus** audio CD for **Units 5b, 7b** and **8a. Unit 5b** also contains a useful checklist for planning short talks.
Part Three **(Collaborative task)**	**Units 2b, 3a, 5b, 6b, 7a** and **8b** involve a task similar to Part Three of the exam.

The numbers refer to the different parts of the Reading, Writing and Listening Tests. For Writing Test Part Two practice, candidates are asked to write either a letter (L) or a report (R) or both (L /R). Two exercises for the same part of the examination are indicated by (2) on the grid. The paler shaded boxes refer to practice tasks which are not exactly examination exercises but practise relevant skills.

Unit		READING						WRITING		LISTENING		
		1	2	3	4	5	6	1	2	1	2*	3
1a	Work roles								R		◱	
1b	Company structures								R			■
	Self-study				■		■					
	Exam practice	■				■						
2a	Stocks & shares							■				
2b	Mergers & acquisitions			■					■	■		
	Self-study				■			■				
	Exam practice		■			■	2					
3a	Trade fairs								L			
3b	Entering a market								L	■		
	Self-study					■						
	Exam practice			■					L			
4a	The future of work	■										■
4b	e-business							■			■	
	Self-study				■							
	Exam practice				■				■	■		
Exam focus												
5a	Staff motivation								R		◱	
5b	Recruitment		■						L			
	Self-study						■					
	Exam practice	■				■						
6a	Corporate culture								■			■
6b	Cultural diversity		■						L			
	Self-study				■			■				
	Exam practice			■	■	■			R/L			
7a	Industrial espionage											
7b	Business ethics										■	
	Self-study					■						
	Exam practice		■				■		L/R			
8a	Global brands			■					R			
8b	Global sourcing	■							R			■
	Self-study				■			2				
	Exam practice				■					■	■	■

* Part Two of the Listening Test consists of two parts.

Questions and answers

I have never taught an examination class before. Can you give me any advice?

The main difference with examination classes is that your objectives are especially clear. You have a syllabus and a certain amount of time to teach it in. Plan the course as a whole but set short-term objectives to check that you are on schedule. Do not fall behind your schedule; overloading students close to the exam will not compensate for bad planning at the start.

You need to be realistic about timing. You have a lot to do to get through the examination syllabus; if you do other things just for interest, you may run out of time. You will need to manage carefully any time spent going over homework in class. You should also be prepared for a lot of marking of written work.

Give your students a mock test before the examination. If course length permits, a preliminary mock examination just before the final entry date also gives students feedback on likely performance before they commit their time and money by entering for the examination. In addition, it will encourage them to revise seriously if necessary.

The best way to familiarise yourself with the examination is to do a past paper. It can also be very helpful to use the Speaking Test preparation pack to show students a complete speaking exam. This pack, as well as past papers, can be ordered directly from Cambridge ESOL.

Can I depart from the book or do I need to follow it exactly?

It is sensible to follow the order of the book (with the exception of Exam focus) if there is no particular reason not to; the sequence has been planned carefully to lead students towards success in the examination. However, the syllabus leading to the examination may not correspond exactly to your students' needs: they may have particular strengths and weaknesses or need specific language for their jobs in addition to general business-related language for the examination. If time permits, tailor the course to the interests and needs of your students.

I'm American. Do I have to teach British English?

Any material needs to be internally consistent and, as Cambridge BEC is a British examination, British English has been chosen as the norm for this book. However, there is a range of nationalities on the audio CD and candidates can use British English, American English, Australian English – or any other native speaker variety – as long as they are consistent. Both American and British English are accepted in the writing section, however, candidates must be consistent. If they start with one variety of English, they should use it throughout. Therefore, teachers should simply teach the language they usually speak.

There's a lot of self-study in the book but my students don't have time for homework.

You need to point out to students that taking an examination course is a commitment; examination courses tend to be intensive and demanding. Make it clear to students that the Self-study and Examination practice sections are essential for recycling and internalising the language presented in the book and for providing adequate examination practice.

My Cambridge BEC students all work for the same company. Some of the pairwork activities won't work with them.

If a speaking activity is irrelevant for your students, adapt it to create a reason for speaking. For example, change the task so that there is an information gap. Or adapt the task to provide an outcome, e.g. ask to agree on a ranking or to present the results of their discussion formally to the rest of the class.

My students are pre-experience. They can't talk about their job or company because they haven't got one.

Once again some of the speaking activities in the book may need to be adapted. Many of the activities involve giving personal opinions and, with a little adaptation, can be done by anybody. For the activities involving companies, the teacher could ask students to talk about companies they know. (This may involve using information about famous companies in the book or asking students to speak about famous local or national companies. It may even involve asking students to do research and find out information before the lesson.)

I have only one student taking Cambridge BEC. Is the book suitable for 1:1 lessons?

Yes – obviously with a little adaptation of some of the oral activities.

Do I have to use the whole book or can I concentrate on the exam practice?

Unlike more general Business English material, this book has been designed to provide extensive preparation for the Cambridge BEC examination. The core units are essential for developing skills – and training students in effective examination techniques.

My students like to talk a lot. Will they find the exam course boring?

Discuss expectations at the start of the course. Fluency practice will be an important and integral part of every lesson but topics will be dictated by the syllabus rather than the students' interests.

Introduction

Unit overview

- **Cambridge Business English Certificate Higher**

  T introduces Ss to the grades and weighting of the parts of the exam.

- **An overview**

  T gives an overview of each part of the exam.

- **Important Cambridge BEC Higher dates**

  T gives Ss some important dates regarding their BEC exam.

- **Preparing for Cambridge BEC Higher**

  T shows the kind of activities Ss will do on their BEC Higher course. Ss decide which they are most and least confident about and which are relevant to their jobs.

- **Quiz: *Pass Cambridge BEC Higher***

  Ss do a quiz in order to familiarise themselves with the *Pass Cambridge BEC Higher* book.

- **Helping yourself succeed**

  Ss consider ways in which they can improve their English skills outside lessons.

Cambridge Business English Certificate Higher

1   This unit assumes that T and Ss already know each other. However, if this is the first time that T and Ss have met, 'getting to know you' type activities may be necessary before doing the unit.

2   **Warmer (books closed):** T writes *Cambridge Business English Certificate Higher* on the board and asks Ss what they expect from the course. T elicits answers related to each word, e.g. *Business* – typical business-related vocabulary, business correspondence; *English* – grammar, general vocabulary, listening practice, speaking practice; *Certificate* – exam preparation.

3   Ss open their books and read the information about Cambridge BEC Higher. T takes Ss through the information about the grades, certificates and results statements.

An overview

4   T briefly outlines the different parts of the exam, using the table. T reassures Ss that the course will provide practice in all four skills. T shows Ss the **Contents** pages of the book to indicate the coverage of reading, writing, listening and speaking listed in the skills column.

   (!)   T need not go into too much depth about the content of the book at this stage. When Ss do a quiz about the book later in this unit, they will discover how the book can help them to prepare for the exam.

Important Cambridge BEC Higher dates

5   Before the lesson, T should find out the Cambridge BEC Higher session dates. In addition, T needs to know the enrolment date fixed by the exam centre. This will be, of course, several weeks before the exam. T tells Ss the various dates, which Ss should write in the boxes. It is impossible to be specific about the Speaking Test at this stage. Ss should, however, be warned to keep weekends free within the period specified. It is essential that all Ss make a record of this information and that any Ss subsequently joining the course also receive this information.

Preparing for Cambridge BEC Higher

6   Ss focus on what the exam involves, how *Pass Cambridge BEC Higher* can help them and what else they can do to prepare for the exam.

   Ex ❶: Ss read the Reading, Writing, Listening, Speaking and Language activities they are going to do on the course. T may wish at this stage to show Ss an example of a Past Paper to illustrate the different parts of the exam. Ss discuss which two activities they are most confident about and which two they are least confident about. T can reassure Ss that the course will provide plenty of training / practice in the areas they feel least confident about.

7   **Ex ❷:** Ss discuss which of the areas are useful for their current job or may be useful in the future. T may need to point out the relevance of some activities (e.g. although the short talk in Part Three of the Speaking Test is much shorter than a standard presentation, the skills covered on the course, such as planning short talks effectively, are very useful).

Quiz: *Pass Cambridge BEC Higher*

8   **Ex ❶:** To introduce Ss to *Pass Cambridge BEC Higher*, T asks Ss to answer the questions by referring to their books. T may wish to ask Ss to work in teams or set a time limit. Alternatively, the exercise could be set as homework.

1	*Unit 6a*	2	*Unit 8a*
3	*Unit 3b*	4	*Audioscript of Unit 5b,*
5	*Unit 1a, Unit 2a, Unit 5a, Unit 7b,*		*page 142*
	Exam focus: Writing	6	*Unit 2b*
7	*Unit 1b*	8	*Unit 6b*
9	*Exam focus*	10	*Unit 2a*
11	*Unit 2b Self-study*	12	*Exam focus: Writing*

9   In feedback, T ensures that Ss are aware of all the sections of the book. T points out that all the double units are followed by **Self-study** and **Exam practice**. The **Self-study** section contains exercises for consolidation/review purposes, which may be set as homework.

T also points out that the core units and the **Self-study** sections contain some exam-related tasks. The exercises in the **Exam practice** sections provide additional practice to ensure coverage of all parts of the exam.

T also ensures Ss are aware of the **Exam focus** section. T tells Ss that they will refer to this section in more detail nearer the exam. T points out that at the back of the book Ss can find **Audioscripts** and the **Answer key**.

10   T focuses Ss' attention on the **Optional tasks** which come at the end of most units. These tasks are optional activities, which are designed to link the lesson with the outside world. In many cases these tasks also practise exam skills such as report writing. T should be aware that these tasks are not included in the **Contents** pages or the grid in the T's guide which summarises the exam practice in the book.

Helping yourself succeed

11   **Ex ❶:** Ss complete the diagram with ideas for improving their English skills outside lessons. In feedback, T highlights those activities which could help Ss in the exam and adds further suggestions, for example, recording a short part of a TV programme, such as the News, and noting down all the names and numbers mentioned and what they refer to. This would be very useful practice for all three parts of the Listening Test, particularly Part One, which requires Ss to listen for specific words and numbers.

Unit la Work roles

Objectives:	To enable Ss to talk about their jobs and duties
	To enable Ss to write reports
	To practise reading for specific information
	To practise listening for gist and specific information
	To review the present simple and present continuous

Unit overview

- **Describing work roles**

Speaking	Ss exchange brief job descriptions.
Reading 1	Ss read about WorkSet and explain the use of colour. Ss then discuss the differences between two pie charts showing a job brief and an employee's feedback.
Language	Ss match verbs with WorkSet colours and think of further verbs.
Listening	Ss listen to five speakers talk about their jobs and decide what each speaker would like to improve (*Listening Test Part Two*).
Language	Ss focus on the present simple and present continuous.
Speaking	Ss interview a partner to produce a WorkSet pie chart for their partner's job.

- **Report writing**

Reading 2	Ss read a report about a seminar on team leadership and say how WorkSet was used. Ss then answer comprehension questions.
Writing	Ss focus on report layout and phrases.
	Ss write a report about their own jobs based on WorkSet pie charts (*Writing Test Part Two*).

Describing work roles

1 **Ex ❶**: Ss work in pairs to exchange information about their jobs and responsibilities. T asks one or two Ss to report back to the group.

2 **Ex ❷**: Ss read the brochure extract to find out how WorkSet uses colour to clarify work roles.

> *Suggested answer:*
> *WorkSet allows companies to clarify work roles by classifying different aspects of the job according to colour. Companies can use colour to specify the exact level of responsibility to be given to a number of key tasks. These specifications can be changed as the job changes. Employees can use the same system to give feedback on the job from their point of view, ensuring that job descriptions remain relevant.*

3 **Ex ❸**: Ss look at the pie charts and discuss the differences between them based on the information in the WorkSet extract. T may wish to elicit possible reasons for the disparity. (T discourages Ss from discussing their own jobs and job descriptions at this stage since this forms the basis of **Ex ❼**.)

> *Suggested answer:*
> *According to the manager's brief, about half of the employee's time should be spent taking personal responsibility for meeting objectives (yellow work). However, the employee feels that this is not the case. Blue work (i.e. work carried out in a prescribed way) is double the amount envisaged in the brief. As can be seen from the grey, white and pink segments, the employee also perceives him/herself to be involved in certain activities outside the job brief. While the small amount of white (creative) work appears to be positive, the pink time serves no useful purpose. Moreover, the incidental grey work which the employee is asked to do in addition to his/her job may be detracting from the core yellow work.*

4 **Ex ❹**: T asks Ss to assign a colour to each verb. Ss may need to look at the extract again first.

> *schedule – yellow*   *support – green*
> *operate – blue*   *design – yellow*
> *co-operate – orange*   *assist – green*
> *participate – orange*   *comply – blue*
> *decide – yellow*   *follow – blue*

T then elicits at least one more verb for each core colour.

> *Suggested answer:*
> *blue – carry out, execute*   *green – aid, cover*
> *yellow – plan, research*   *orange – take part, brainstorm*

−1.05

Ex ❺: T introduces Ss to Listening Test Part Two. T then asks Ss to read through the list of improvements and think of the words or phrases they would expect to hear connected with each one. For example, for *more responsibility*, Ss might expect to hear phrases such as *my boss should delegate more, greater decision-making powers*.

T may like to ask Ss to assign WorkSet colours to the different tasks the speakers describe.

1 H   2 D   3 B   4 E   5 A

> **Exam focus: Listening Test Part Two**
>
> Candidates listen to five short topic-related extracts and complete two tasks, which may involve identifying any combination of the following for each extract: speaker, topic, function, opinion or feelings. The five extracts are heard twice. Both tasks test candidates' ability to listen for gist and specific information.
>
> Candidates should be aware that each extract contains both a Task One answer and a Task Two answer. Some candidates may prefer to deal with Task One during the first listening and Task Two during the second listening, or they may choose to attempt the two tasks simultaneously. For each task, they have a list of eight options to choose from. Incorrect options are included in the recordings in order to distract unwary candidates.
>
> *This exercise differs from the exam in that here there is only one task. In the exam itself candidates have to do two tasks for each extract.*

6   Ex ❻: T refers Ss to the example sentences. Ss then look through the audioscript to find further examples of the present simple and present continuous and discuss how they are used. Ss should be encouraged to categorise examples of the tenses rather than discuss every occurrence separately. (See the end of this unit for further information on the present simple and present continuous.)

Present simple and present continuous forms are bolded in T's audioscript.

7   Ex ❼: Ss work in pairs and use WorkSet to produce a pie chart describing their partner's job. T points out that Ss should use both the core and employee feedback colours. T should encourage Ss to think about their work in an average week rather than in a single day.

Report writing

8   Ex ❶: T asks Ss to read the report and decide how Barrie Watson used WorkSet. T can accept brief answers only as Ss will focus on the details of how he used WorkSet in the questions in **Ex ❷.**

Suggested answer:
Barrie Watson used WorkSet to ascertain that Ekstrom Team Leaders had different perceptions of the precise level of responsibility to be allocated to each of their key tasks. He then helped the company to use the WorkSet colours to select which level was most appropriate for each task and to communicate its expectations to the Team Leaders.

9 **Ex ❷:** Ss read the report again and answer the questions.

> 1   To explain how they saw their roles.
> 2   Leaders had different perceptions of their roles.
> 3   To communicate the most appropriate approach to a series of key tasks.
> 4   Skills can be developed; attributes (i.e. the qualities people are born with) cannot.
> 5   It can set up assessment centres to screen applicants and team leaders.

10 **Ex ❸:** T focuses on the structure and layout of the report, drawing Ss' attention to the overall title and the headings of the sections. T then asks Ss to read the report again and identify useful phrases for writing reports.

> **Introduction:** *The aim of this report is to ...*
> **Findings:** *This disparity clearly showed ...*
> **Conclusions:** *It is clear that ...*
> **Recommendations:** *We strongly recommend that ...*

(!) The reports Ss write in the exam tend to be less business-like and more personal than the Belbin report. However, it is useful for Ss to focus on standard report layout and language before they write exam-style reports.

11 As Ss may be asked in the exam to write a report with recommendations, T may wish to spend a few minutes focusing on the possible structures following phrases such as *It is suggested* ... T ensures that Ss realise that *suggest* is never followed by *to*. (See the end of this unit for further information on making recommendations.)

12 **Ex ❹:** T introduces Ss to Writing Test Part Two (Report). T may wish to ask Ss to prepare a detailed plan in class showing how they intend to organise their ideas before they write a report for homework. Alternatively, T may like to ask Ss to prepare the pie charts in class and discuss them briefly before completing the written task as homework.

T should refer Ss to the three bullet points to remind them to plan and organise their writing carefully.

T points out that Ss will probably write the report in the first person. (See the end of this unit for a sample report written in this way.) Alternatively, T may wish to ask Ss to write in the third person. This choice will have an impact on the language Ss use: a report written in the third person is likely to sound more formal and impersonal and is more likely to include the phrases taught in the unit.

Exam focus: Writing Test Part Two (Report)

For Writing Test Part Two, candidates write a 200–250 word proposal, piece of business correspondence or report. All the points in the rubric must be included in the answer. To generate the range of language required at this level, the task input is broad and non-specific, which means that a reasonably high background knowledge is needed by the candidate. To ensure that no candidate is disadvantaged a choice of tasks is given. The task tests the ability to produce an appropriate piece of extended directed writing.

For the report, candidates are expected to plan, organise and present their ideas clearly. Reports should be clearly set out, with paragraphs, headings (e.g. *Introduction, Findings, Conclusion*) and bullet points where appropriate. All reports are expected to have a title.

Present simple and present continuous

The uses of the present simple and present continuous which appear in the audioscript are as follows.

Present simple
- **To refer to permanent or long-term situations:**
  *I **work** for the UK subsidiary of a Japanese company.*
- **To refer to regular actions:**
  *I **produce** technical documents.*
- **To refer to states:**
  *I **have** a lot more responsibility now.*
- **To refer to future time in subordinate clauses:**
  *I always have to consult him before I **can** make even the smallest alteration.*
- **As part of a conditional clause:**
  *If something **needs** doing, then I think whoever's available should do it.*

Present continuous
- **To refer to temporary situations:**
  ***I'm travelling** around Europe a lot.*
- **To refer to current activities:**
  *I'm a temp and **I'm working** as a PA for a law firm in London just now.*
- **To refer to an activity happening around a particular time:**
  *Especially when you're **starting** a new job ...*
- **To emphasise that an activity is ongoing:**
  *Everyone's still **clocking** in and out at the same time.*

In addition to these uses, T may wish to encourage an understanding of the fundamental difference between simple and continuous forms.

The simple form expresses the idea of the state or action as basic information or a whole. It can be thought of as the neutral form, when the speaker has no reason to emphasise, or chooses not to emphasise, a time element.

The key idea of the continuous form is that the speaker is relating the action to a specific time, either now or in the future. The speaker may choose to use the continuous form to suggest that the situation has changed or will change.

Making recommendations

Particular attention should be paid to structures following *suggest, recommend* and *advise.*

It is suggested ~~to set up~~ assessment centres.
*It is suggested that Ekstrom **should set up** assessment centres.*
*It is suggested that Ekstrom **sets up** assessment centres.*
*It is suggested that Ekstrom **set up** assessment centres.**

*The subjunctive is sometimes used in a formal style when expressing the idea that something is important or desirable. The third person singular takes no **-s** in the present tense; the form looks like the infinitive. The subjunctive has only a limited use in contemporary English.

Ss need to ensure that they use a consistent style across a document, whether they are writing formally, neutrally or informally.

Report writing Ex ❹:

Reassessment of job description: Sue Pearson (PR Dept.)

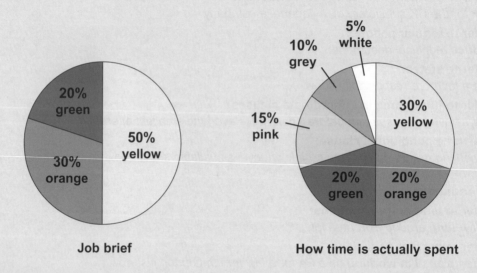

Job brief   How time is actually spent

Introduction
This report sets out to use WorkSet colours to assess the accuracy of my job description as PR Officer and to suggest a number of changes.

Findings
It is clear that there is a difference between the way the company views the job and the reality as I perceive it. Firstly, a number of areas which demand a significant proportion of my time are not mentioned in the official job brief. The segment on the pie chart which provides most cause for concern is the pink sector; this relates to my attendance at a number of meetings to which I can contribute little. Another significant area is the grey segment; this refers to the unscheduled time which I spend sorting out computer problems. I feel that these activities are hampering my core work. As can be seen from the pie charts, the time I spend actively working to meet the goals agreed with my line manager is less than envisaged.

Conclusions
The above discrepancies clearly indicate that my current job brief is inaccurate.

Recommendations
I would recommend that my official job brief should be updated using the WorkSet colours. It would also be valuable to consider the proportion of non-core colours in the pie chart and to investigate whether work in these areas could be carried out by someone else more suited to these tasks.

Unit Ib Company structure

Objectives:	To enable Ss to talk about company structure
	To practise reading and listening for specific information
	To review the past simple, present perfect simple and present perfect continuous

Unit overview

- **Types of company structure**

Speaking	Ss look at three diagrams showing company structures and say what kind of companies they could be.
Reading	Ss read a newspaper article about company structures and list the advantages and disadvantages of each structure. Ss then answer comprehension questions.
Speaking	Ss discuss the structure of their company.

- **Flexible working**

Listening	Ss listen to a manager of a manufacturing company talk about changes to the retirement age and summarise the programme he is discussing.
	Ss listen again and answer multiple-choice comprehension questions (*Listening Test Part Three*).
Language	Ss focus on the past simple, present perfect simple and present perfect continuous.
Speaking	Ss use a questionnaire to assess the suitability of their partner being redeployed in a training or mentoring role.
Writing	Ss write a proposal assessing the suitability of themselves or their partner to be redeployed in a training or mentoring role. (*Writing Test Part Two*).
Optional task	Ss visit Asda's recruitment website and identify how the company values its employees and builds team spirit within the workforce.

Types of company structure

1 **Ex ❶:** Ss discuss what kind of company structure they think is represented by each diagram.

 Suggested answer:
A   Large established company. Hierarchical pyramid structure.
B   Small company (owner manager). Flat management structure.
C   Flexible company with project-based teams.

2 **Ex ❷:** T asks Ss to read the article about company structure and label each diagram. Ss use the text to draw up a list of the advantages and disadvantages of each structure. To save time, T may wish to ask Ss to work in pairs and assign one structure per pair.

    A ***Hierarchical organisation***
      Advantages: *High level of control.*
      Disadvantages: *Workers lack the authority and motivation to improve processes. Management's response time is slow. Only suitable for stable business environments.*

    B ***Entrepreneurial organisation***
      Advantages: *Totally centralised authority and direct contact between owner and employees ensure responsiveness to external changes.*
      Disadvantages: *Only suitable for small companies.*

    C ***Information age organisation***
      Advantages: *Allows speed of response within a large complex structure. Retains control but gives quick access to information. Employees can constantly refine their actions and strategies. Organisational control is dynamic.*
      Disadvantages: *Although IT makes all these advantages possible, it cannot motivate people to use the information they have.*

3 **Ex ❸:** Ss re-read the article in order to find the answers to the questions.

    1 *Operating processes are concerned with how a company produces and sells its products and services. Management processes are concerned with how a company directs and controls these operations.*
    2 *Jobs are standardised and separated into sequential steps which are carried out under direct supervision.*
    3 *There is daily personal interaction between the owner and employees.*
    4 *Access to information alone cannot motivate people to use that information on behalf of the organisation. Organisations need to ensure that the information is used by managers and employees to accomplish the same goals.*

4 **Ex ❹:** Ss discuss which of the structures described in the article is most like the organisation they work for. T may wish to encourage Ss to think in terms of their own department as well as the company as a whole and say whether they have experienced any of the advantages or disadvantages mentioned in the article.

Flexible working

5 **Ex ❶:** Ss listen and decide if Don McNally is looking forward to the changes and why.

> **Suggested answer:**
> *He sees the changes as being essential for the future of the company and if handled properly, will be good for both motivation and productivity.*

6 **Ex ❷:** T introduces Ss to Listening Test Part Three. T asks Ss to read through the questions before listening, pointing out that the answers will appear in the same order. When checking the answers, T may wish to ask Ss to identify where the answers appeared in the audioscript.

> *1 B   2 C   3 A   4 B   5 A   6 C   7 B   8 A*

Exam focus: Listening Test Part Three

Candidates listen to a 3–4 minute recording of two or three speakers and answer eight multiple-choice questions. The recording is heard twice. This task tests ability to listen for specific information.

The questions follow the order of the recording and are clearly signposted by the speaker(s). Incorrect options are included in the recording in order to distract unwary candidates.

---

7 **Ex ❸:** T refers Ss to the example sentences. Ss then look through the audioscript to find further examples of the past simple, present perfect simple and present perfect continuous and discuss how they are used. To save time, T may wish to assign one tense per pair or small group. Ss should be encouraged to categorise examples of the tenses rather than discuss every occurrence separately. (See the end of this unit for further information on the past simple, present perfect simple and present perfect continuous.)

> *Past simple, present perfect simple and present perfect continuous forms are bolded in Ts audioscript.*

8 **Ex ❹:** Ss work in pairs and take turns to assess if their partner would be suitable for redeployment in either a training or mentoring role. T asks Ss to consider other factors that would make someone a good trainer or mentor. Make sure Ss understand the difference between training (more formal with clear objectives) and mentoring (informal and with no obligation from either party).

9 Ex ❺: This exercise practises the skills needed for Writing Test Part Two. T may wish to ask Ss to prepare a detailed plan in class showing how they intend to organise their ideas before they write a report for homework. When setting the task, T may wish to refer Ss back to Unit 1a for useful report phrases. T reminds Ss, where necessary, that the report should be about their own job, not their partner's.

If Ss do the writing task in class, T may wish to ask Ss to exchange reports in pairs and give each other feedback using the **Writing Test Assessment Sheet** on page 78 of the Student's Book. Before the lesson, T should have made photocopies of the Assessment Sheet for Ss to use. (See the end of this unit for a sample report.)

⚠ T should ensure that the Assessment Sheet has been presented clearly to Ss. (See T's notes for the **How to succeed** section of **Exam focus: Writing** for further information.)

Exam focus: Writing Test Part Two (Report)

For Writing Test Part Two, candidates write a 200–250 word proposal, piece of business correspondence or report. All the points in the rubric must be included in the answer. To generate the range of language required at this level, the task input is broad and non-specific, which means that a reasonably high background knowledge is needed by the candidate. To ensure that no candidate is disadvantaged a choice of tasks is given. The task tests the ability to produce an appropriate piece of extended directed writing.

For the report, candidates are expected to plan, organise and present their ideas clearly. Reports should be clearly set out, with paragraphs, headings (e.g. *Introduction, Findings, Conclusion*) and bullet points where appropriate. All reports are expected to have a title.

---

10 Ex ❻: This is the first Optional Task in the book, the aim of which is to give Ss an additional task (to be done as homework) which will link the lesson with the outside world.

When setting the Task, T may wish to elicit the sort of considerations the Ss expect to see mentioned by Asda. T points out to Ss that it may be necessary for them to look at more than one web-page in order to complete the task satisfactorily.

Past simple, present perfect simple and present perfect continuous

The uses of the past simple, present perfect simple and present perfect continuous which appear in the audioscript are as follows.

Past simple

- **To refer to actions started and finished in the past:**
  Our research showed that the overwhelming majority of requests to continue working were accepted.
- **To refer to a definite time in the past:**
  We started looking at this as a possible solution last year.

Present perfect simple

- **To refer to actions started in the past but unfinished:**
  Well, we have had a reasonable degree of flexibility in retirement age for a long time now.
- **To refer to an indefinite time in the past:**
  There has been some reluctance on the part of individuals.
- **To refer to past action with present consequences:**
  Absenteeism has decreased ...
- **To refer to recent actions:**
  We have already developed teams where ...

Present perfect continuous

- **To refer to actions started in the past and continuing into the future:**
  ... as older engineers have been gradually handing over decision making to their younger colleagues.
- **To refer to repeated or continuous actions in the past with present consequences:**
  The young have been acquiring the working habits of their older colleagues.

In addition to these uses, T may wish to encourage an understanding of the fundamental differences between the three forms.

The past simple is used to talk about completed actions and facts related to past time.

Both forms of the present perfect contain the idea of a link between past and present time and in some cases it is possible to use either form.
e.g.   *He's **worked** here for three years.*   ✔
         *He's **been working** here for three years.*   ✔

However, Ss need to be aware that there is a difference in emphasis between the two: the present perfect simple focuses on the completion or result of an activity (the product) whereas the present perfect continuous focuses on the continuity of an activity (the process).
e.g.   *I've **written** the sales report.*   ✔
         *I've **been** writing letters.*   ✔

The continuous form of the present perfect is not possible with certain verbs.
e.g.   *The new manager **has arrived.***   ✔
         *The new manager **has been arriving**.*   ✗

Flexible working Ex ❺:

Sample answer: *(239 words)*

Resource Planning Manager: Assessment of suitability for redeployment

Introduction
The purpose of this report is to assess the suitability of my position as a Resource Planning Manager for redeployment in a training or mentoring role, before taking retirement.

Findings
My work is largely office based, with some visits to production facilities on an irregular basis. Much of my working day is spent in meetings with junior staff, delegating tasks and overseeing the planning of workloads. Communication is key to my current position and I am often consulted by managers of other departments, drawing on my expertise, developed over more than twenty years experience.

As regards health, I have no known medical conditions that would prevent me from continuing to work in a full time capacity for the foreseeable future. I would like to remain with the company, although would prefer to reduce my workload over a period of time.

Conclusion
I am a highly skilled and experienced member of the management team. Over the years I have built a network of contacts throughout the industry, and have proved myself to be a valuable asset to the company. I believe my colleagues, especially the less experienced, have come to rely on my knowledge and help on a daily basis.

Recommendations
I would suggest that I should be considered for a training role for a trial period. After this time, further consultation should take place in order to reassess the situation.

Unit 2a Stocks and shares

Objectives:	To enable Ss to talk about financial trends
	To enable Ss to describe trends in writing
	To practise listening for specific information
	To review language of similarity and difference
Materials needed:	Cards **six cards; one set of cards per pair to be photocopied**

Unit overview

- ### Share prices

Speaking	Ss discuss where they can find out about a company's share price.
Reading	Ss read an extract from a stock market listing and match definitions with headings.
Speaking	Ss discuss the popularity of investing in shares in their country.

- ### Market trends

Listening 1	Ss listen to a television report about share prices of retail companies and summarise the general trend. Ss listen again and answer multiple-choice comprehension questions (*Listening Test Part Three*).
Speaking	Ss discuss whether they would invest in retail shares.

- ### Describing graphs

Speaking	Ss describe a graph using the words on cards.
Listening 2	Ss listen to a description of the graph and re-order the cards.
Language	Ss focus on trends language.
	Ss focus on the language of similarity and difference.
Writing	Ss write a description of a graph comparing two companies' share prices (*Writing Test Part One*).
Optional task	Ss begin a fantasy stock market investment game, which can run throughout the course.

Share prices

1 **Ex ❶**: T asks Ss where they can find information about share prices in their country.

Suggested answer:
financial pages of newspapers, Internet, financial pages of Teletext

2 **Ex ❷**: T asks Ss to look at an extract from a stock market listing and match the letters with the definitions. T may wish to point out at this stage that 'FT500' stands for the Financial Times 500 and is a list of the world's largest companies ranked by market capitalisation. The prices are in US dollars.

1 B   2 D   3 F   4 A   5 C   6 E

Supplementary activity

T may like to ask Ss to find some figures to check their understanding of the terms.

a   What was the price of Amazon shares at the close of trading?*(234.78)*
b   What was the total market value of 3M? *($57,103m)*
c   What was the price/earnings ratio of AKBank shares? *(10.18)*
d   What was Accenture's lowest share price? *(43.06)*
e   Which company's shares showed the biggest change in share price? *(Anadarko)*

---

3 **Ex ❸**: T asks Ss how common investing in shares is in their country. Ss then discuss why individuals and companies might invest in shares.

Suggested answer:
Individuals might invest in shares: *to make a quick profit from privatisations, to get a better return on long-term investment than in a traditional savings scheme, as part of a benefits package (share options), to become eligible for shareholder perks, to support a company they like*

Companies might invest in shares: *to avoid paying tax, to reinvest profits, to increase company pension funds, to have a participating interest in other companies, (in stock swaps with other companies, in hostile takeover bids etc.), to consolidate strategic alliances*

Market trends

4 **Ex ❶**: T tells Ss that they are going to listen to a report about the share prices of retail companies. Before listening, T asks Ss to predict how they think shares will have performed. Ss then listen to check their predictions. (T emphasises that Ss are listening for how retail **share prices** have performed rather than the companies themselves in more general terms.)

Suggested answer:
Retail share prices were quite strong a year ago, but recently they have been quite volatile and share prices have fallen.

5 **Ex ❷:** This exercise practises the skills needed for Listening Test Part Three. T asks Ss to read through the questions before listening. When checking the answers, T may wish to ask Ss to identify where the answers appeared in the audioscript.

1 C	2 A	3 B	4 C	5 A	6 B	7 C	8 C

> **Exam focus: Listening Test Part Three**
>
> Candidates listen to a 3–4 minute recording of two or three speakers and answer eight multiple-choice questions. The recording is heard twice. This task tests ability to listen for specific information.
>
> The questions follow the order of the recording and are clearly signposted by the speaker(s). Incorrect options are included in the recording in order to distract unwary candidates.

6 **Ex ❸:** Ss say whether or not they would be prepared to invest in retail shares and explain why.

Describing graphs

7 **Ex ❶:** Before the lesson, T should have photocopied cards from the back of the T's Book. T introduces Ss to Writing Test Part One. T then asks Ss to look at the graph and checks that they understand what it represents. T gives each pair or group of Ss a set of the cards and asks Ss to describe the graph **using the exact words** on their cards. This is simply a prediction exercise for the listening in **Ex ❷** so T should not allow Ss to spend too much time on this activity. T should ask Ss to leave the cards on the table in the order they have been used in preparation for the next exercise.

> **Exam focus: Writing Test Part One**
>
> Candidates write a 120–140 word report describing trends. The task tests concise writing skills.
>
> Candidates are expected to describe, compare and contrast information presented visually, in the form of graphs, bar charts and pie charts. Candidates should use appropriate language of trends and must be concise in order to avoid exceeding the strict word limit.

8 **Ex ❷:** T asks Ss to listen to the description of the graph and to re-order the cards as they hear the words. (The answers are also bolded in T's audioscript.)

a dip	collapse	fluctuations	fallen	recovered	a high

9 T then refers Ss to the audioscript so that they can check how the words were used. The speaker does not simply list small movements but tries to give the listener a feeling for the general trends, supporting more general comments with details (e.g. *... after Christmas there were some fluctuations. The price eventually recovered, even reaching a high towards the end of February*). T should also point out how the speaker does not simply use past simple and present perfect verbs but makes the description more interesting: a participle is used to comment on a past simple verb (e.g. *It then finally rallied, getting ...*); the speaker changes perspective using the past perfect (e.g. *... by the middle of March the price had fallen to a low of ...*); nouns are used as well as verbs (e.g. *We can expect a dip ...*). This will be important for Writing Test Part One, in which Ss have to describe and compare trends.

10 **Ex ❸:** In this exercise Ss will focus on the language used to describe graphs, which is particularly useful for Writing Test Part One. T asks Ss to search through the audioscript for examples of the points related to describing graphs. To save time, T may wish to assign one category per pair or small group. T should direct Ss' attention to the general nouns related to trends. T emphasises that in order to do well in Writing Test Part One, Ss should be able to demonstrate a similarly rich range of vocabulary.

> *Suggested answer:*
> *Adjectives: typical attractive, stable, predictable*
> *Adverbs: fairly, reasonably, finally, slightly*
> *Verbs: recovered, fell, reaching, fallen, getting back, settling*
> *Nouns: rise, a high, a low, a dip, price collapse, fluctuations*
> *Prepositions with time phrases: over the last three months, by the middle of March, in April, after Christmas*
> *Prepositions with figures: from, to around, just over, down from*

11 T refers Ss to the **Don't forget!** section. T points out that in Part One of the Writing Test, Ss are expected to be able to compare and contrast as well as describe visual information. T encourages Ss to note down any additional words and phrases for describing similarity and difference as they come across them during their course.

12 **Ex ❹:** Ss write a 120–140 word report comparing the share prices of Marks and Spencer plc and The Carphone Warehouse. T may wish to ask Ss to describe and compare the graphs orally in class before they write a report for homework. If Ss do the writing task in class, T may wish to ask Ss to exchange reports in pairs and give each other feedback.

Describing graphs Ex ❹:

> *Sample answer:*   *(139 words)*
> *The share prices of both Marks and Spencer plc and The Carphone Warehouse reached about 380p in November. Yet, whilst M&S plc shares had fallen from 400p, those of CW's had risen from an earlier low of 350p. Both fell slowly over the next few months, although CW's were more volatile, and showed some signs of recovery, only to dip again.*
>
> *Both reached their low at about the same time, with M&S plc's falling to 330p, and CW's being approximately 30 points higher. M&S plc recovered slowly, climbing back to 400p towards the end of this period. There were one or two sudden rises, followed by equally sudden falls in CW's share price, but they generally remained stable at the 370p mark throughout March. Prices then rose sharply to 400p, where they stayed for the remainder of the period.*

13 **Ex ❺:** Once again, the Optional Task is designed to link the lesson with the outside world. T can ask Ss to report on the progress of their investment on an ongoing basis. At a later stage in the course, T may wish to ask Ss to write a report summarising the success of their investment. T should ensure that, for the purposes of comparison, Ss all use the same index throughout.

Unit 2b Mergers and acquisitions

Objectives:	To enable Ss to talk about mergers and acquisitions
	To practise reading and listening for specific information
	To practise a collaborative speaking task
	To review aspects of cohesion

Unit overview

- **Understanding mergers**

Speaking	Ss discuss why companies merge and problems which might arise.
Reading	Ss read an article about mergers and acquisitions and decide whether there are ever any benefits. Ss then answer multiple-choice comprehension questions (*Reading Test Part Three*).
Language	Ss focus on linking devices.
Speaking	Ss talk about a recent merger in their country.

- **A merger of equals**

Listening	Ss listen to a talk about trends in mergers and acquisitions and complete notes (*Listening Test Part One*).
Speaking	Ss discuss a company they would like to merge with or acquire and the resulting benefits (*Speaking Test Part Three*).
Optional task	Ss write a brief profile of a recent merger.

Understanding mergers

1 **Ex ❶:** T elicits reasons why companies merge with or acquire other companies. T then asks Ss what problems can arise. T may wish to put these ideas on the board to see how many of them are mentioned when Ss do **Ex ❷**.

>
> *Suggested answer:*
> **Possible reasons:** *pursuit of monopoly, financial engineering (asset stripping), pressure from investors, creating opportunity for growth*
>
> **Possible problems:** *bad debts, companies not integrated successfully, managerial overconfidence, job losses and lack of investment*

2 The headlines are for visual effect only and are not closely related to the exercises. However, if Ss recognise the companies mentioned, T may wish to ask Ss to speculate on the reasons for the mergers/ takeovers.

3 **Ex ❷:** Ss read the article and complete the table with the successes and problems mentioned.

Successes	Problems
	Lloyds/HBOS: bad debt
	RBS/ABN: bad debt
	HSBC/Household: bad debt
	RBS/NatWest: increased value
BP: major world company	*Integration not completed*
Vodafone/Mannesmann	*No value in shares*
Glaxo/SmithKline	*No value in shares*

4 **Ex ❸:** T introduces Ss to Reading Test Part Three and emphasises that the answers appear in the text in the same order as the questions. T asks Ss to read through the questions. Ss then read the text again in more detail to answer the questions and complete the sentences.

	1 B	2 C	3 D	4 B	5 B	6 D

Exam focus: Reading Test Part Three

Candidates read a 500–600 word text and answer six multiple-choice questions. This tests ability to read for specific information.

Candidates read the whole text briefly for general understanding and then read the questions and options. Ss re-read the text and answer the questions they feel sure of. They then concentrate on scanning the text for the answers to the remaining questions. The questions follow the order of the text, which should help Ss narrow down the location of a relevant passage in the text.

---

5 **Ex ❹:** In this exercise Ss will focus on cohesion, an awareness of which is useful for all parts of the Reading and Writing Tests, particularly Reading Test Part Two. T checks that Ss understand the terms used in the exercise and asks them to search through the article for further examples. To save time, T may wish to assign one category per pair or small group. (See the end of this unit for further information on linking.)

Suggested answer:

Linking words and Phrases
Sequencers: is one reason (Para. 10), is another (Para. 11)
Addition: and (Para. 4), What's more (Para. 5)
Contrast: Yet (Para. 5), to the contrary (Para. 8), but (Para. 4 and 10), However (Para. 12)
Purpose: So (Para. 9)

Reference words
Pronouns: it, its, they, his
This: this is almost as bad (Para. 3), this purpose (Para. 11)
These: these companies (Para. 10)
The: the HBOS takeover (Para. 2), the acquisition (Para. 4), the success (Para. 5)

Lexical substitution
Examples of substitution are:
*Royal bank of Scotland (Para. 3) ... **the tiny Scottish upstart** (Para. 5)*
*mergers ... **takeovers** (throughout)*

Relative Clauses
... which similarly holed ... (Para. 3)
... who was formerly ... (Para. 6)
... which allows the corporate landscape ... (Para. 10)
... who seem to be the root ... (Para. 12)

6 **Ex ❺:** Ss briefly discuss the reasons behind a recent merger or acquisition.

A merger of equals

7 **Ex ❶:** T introduces Ss to Listening Test Part One. T then asks Ss to read through the handout and predict what sort of information or word types could be used to complete each sentence. Ss listen and complete the notes.

 These answers are bolded in T's audioscript.

1 economic forecasting	2 spate	3 fall in profitability
4 long-term growth	5 more competitive	6 phase of re-organisation
7 bailed out	8 good sense	9 industry rivals
10 more sustainable	11 more conservatively	12 bidders

> **Exam focus: Listening Test Part One**
>
> Candidates listen to a monologue (or a series of long turns by more than one speaker) and complete each of the gaps in the text with up to three words or a number. There are twelve gaps in total. The recording is heard twice. This task tests the ability to listen for and note specific information.
>
> Candidates have 45 seconds to read through the input before listening and should use the time to think about what might fit in the gaps. The questions follow the order of the recording. Candidates are expected to write the **exact words** used in the recording. Provided that the words written are recognisable, candidates are not penalised for incorrect spelling.

8 After the listening exercise, T may find it useful to discuss the speed at which Ss are expected to write Listening Test Part One answers. If Ss mention that they take notes using abbreviations, T should point out that in this exercise their note-taking must be accurate as candidates are expected to write the **exact words** they hear. Therefore, it might be dangerous to write ↑ for *increase* or *prod* for *production* as the candidate might forget the exact word and write a synonym or similar word (e.g. *rose* or *productivity*) when transferring his/her answers.

9 **Ex ❷:** T introduces Ss to Speaking Test Part Three. T should stress the importance of briefly establishing a context at the start of the discussion (e.g. if Ss do not work for the same company, they need to establish who they work for). Ss try to reach agreement on which company to merge with and the benefits that would result. T may wish to assess Ss' performance using the Collaborative Task section of the **Speaking Test Assessment Sheet** on page 83 of the Student's Book.

> **Exam focus: Speaking Test Part Three**
>
> This is a collaborative task. Candidates are required to have a brief guided discussion in pairs or threes. They are given a task sheet which outlines a business situation and the points which need to be discussed and decided together. Candidates have 30 seconds to prepare individually for the discussion.
>
> Candidates should start by establishing a context (e.g. the type of company they work for). They are expected to be able to initiate, respond and turn-take appropriately without intervention by the examiner. Candidates need to be aware that they are expected to move the discussion towards a decision rather than simply discuss various options.

10 **Ex ❸:** Once again, the Optional Task is designed to link the classroom with the real world. T might wish to set a word limit for the profile in order to accustom Ss to writing concisely.

Linking

In order to unite a text, the following cohesive devices may be used.

Linking words and phrases

Ss need to be able to recognise the function of and use a range of linking words and phrases in areas such as addition, contrast, example and ordering. In addition to knowing words and phrases which link ideas, Ss also need to develop a command of phrases which organise and link the text as a whole, e.g. *... is one reason ...*

Reference words

When reading, Ss need to ensure that they understand exactly what reference words such as *it, their* and *this* are referring to. Particular attention should be paid to *this*, which can refer back to one word, a sentence or even a whole paragraph. Ss also need to ensure that their use of reference words is clear in their own writing.

Lexical repetition/substitution

A text can be united by the repetition of the same word (lexical repetition). Alternatively, a different word or phrase can be substituted to refer to the same thing (substitution), e.g. *Royal Bank of Scotland/tiny Scottish upstart*

Relative clauses

Sentences can be linked using relative pronouns (*who, which, that* etc.). In defining relative clauses, no comma is used; the relative clause is necessary in order to make the meaning clear, e.g. *... is another form of industrial structuring which allows the corporate landscape to evolve and change.* In non-defining relative clauses, any information which could be in a separate sentence is separated with commas, e.g. *Lord Browne, who was formerly chief executive of BP, was a classic example of it.*

Unit 3a Trade fairs

Objectives:	To enable Ss to talk about trade fairs
	To enable Ss to write formal business letters
	To practise a collaborative speaking task
	To review the present simple referring to future time
Materials needed:	Cards **six cards; one set of cards per pair to be photocopied**

Unit overview

- **Exhibiting at a trade fair**

Speaking	Ss discuss the benefits of trade fairs for exhibitors and visitors.
Reading 1	Ss read an advertisement for the Festival of Ceramics exhibition and give information about the exhibition, exhibitors and visitors.
Speaking	Ss discuss their objectives for a trade fair and decide where and when they should exhibit (*Speaking Test Part Three*).

- **Replying to an enquiry**

Speaking	Ss discuss what information they would include in a reply to enquiries about an exhibition.
Reading 2	Ss re-order a jumbled letter to form a standard letter of reply and divide it into paragraphs.
	Ss read the complete letter and compare it with their own.
	Ss discuss the organisation of the letter.
Language	Ss focus on the present simple referring to future time.
	Ss focus on standard letter phrases.
Writing	Ss write a letter replying to an enquiry about their company and its products/services (*Writing Test Part Two*).
Optional task	Ss research a trade fair and write a report recommending why their company should exhibit there.

Exhibiting at a trade fair

1   Warmer (optional): T asks Ss about the different ways their company promotes its products/services.

2   Ex ❶: Ss briefly discuss the benefits of trade fairs. To save time, T may wish to ask some Ss to think about the benefits for the exhibitors and others to think about the benefits for the visitors.

> ***Suggested answer:***
> ***Benefits for exhibitors:*** *media exposure for the industry as a whole and for specific companies, an opportunity to show their wares to an interested public, to find out what is happening in the industry and to evaluate the competition*
>
> ***Benefits for visitors:*** *the ease of judging relative standards and prices, an opportunity to find out what is happening in the industry, the convenience of everything in one place, a chance to talk to exhibitors*

3   Ex ❷ Ss read the Festival of Ceramics advertisement and look for information about the exhibition, exhibitors and visitors.

(!)   T may wish to point out that the 'buyers' referred to in the advertisement are not members of the public but professional buyers from the retail sector.

> ***The exhibition:*** *It is called Festival of Ceramics. It exhibits both highly individual ceramic pieces and more practical, mainstream products. The two-day exhibition takes place at the NEC in Birmingham annually. There are also workshops, business seminars and a showcase for new designers.*
>
> ***The exhibitors:*** *over 400 exhibitors are selected to display their new products. Fifty places are kept for new exhibitors.*
>
> ***The visitors:*** *Each exhibition attracts about 30,000 UK and international buyers and suppliers.*

4   Ex ❸: This exercise practises the skills needed for Speaking Test Part Three. Ss establish a context and try to reach agreement on their objectives for the trade fair and where and when they should exhibit. T may wish to assess Ss' performance using the Collaborative Task section of the **Speaking Test Assessment Sheet** on page 83 of the Student's Book.

(!)   T should ensure that the Assessment Sheet has been presented clearly to Ss. (See T's notes for the **How to succeed** section of **Exam focus: Speaking** for further information.)

Exam focus: Speaking Test Part Three

This is a collaborative task. Candidates are required to have a brief guided discussion in pairs or threes. They are given a task sheet which outlines a business situation and the points which need to be discussed and decided together. Candidates have 30 seconds to prepare individually for the discussion.

Candidates should start by establishing a context (e.g. the type of company they work for). They are expected to be able to initiate, respond and turn-take appropriately without intervention by the examiner. Candidates need to be aware that they are expected to move the discussion towards a decision rather than simply discuss various options.

Replying to an enquiry

5 **Ex ❶:** T elicits the type of information Ss think trade fair organisers would include in their standard reply to enquiries.

> ***Suggested answer:***
> *dates, duration, location, size, focus (for trade/public), stand size, cost, facilities (car parking, catering etc.)*

6 **Ex ❷:** Before the lesson, T should have photocopied the jumbled letter from the back of the T's Book. T explains the task and elicits what sort of clues Ss will use to help them order the sentences. These ideas may be put on the board as a reference for Ss as they work through the activity. T puts Ss into pairs or small groups and gives each pair a set of strips. Ss order the strips and then divide the completed letter into paragraphs. When checking the answers, Ss should be encouraged to justify their order. More than one answer is possible.

7 **Ex ❸:** Ss read through the letter and compare it with their own version. T encourages Ss to discuss any differences and the possible reasons behind them. T may also wish to refer Ss back to **Ex ❶** to see which of their ideas were included in the actual letter.

8 **Ex ❹:** In this exercise Ss will focus on features of organisation which will help them in their writing, particularly Writing Test Part Two (Letter). T asks Ss to search through the letter to find examples of the points related to organisation. This exercise is expected to focus Ss on the features which helped them to order the jumbled letter. (See the end of this unit for further information on the organisation of letters.)

> ***Standard letter phrases***
> *These standard phrases probably helped Ss to order the beginning and ending of the letter:*
> *Thank you for your interest ...*
> *As requested, I enclose ...*
> *If you require any further information ... do not hesitate to ...*
> *I look forward to hearing from you*
> *Best wishes*
>
> ***Main points***
> *The writer refers to the reader's request for information before giving information about the Festival of Ceramics. The second and third paragraphs are quite general about the Festival of Ceramics. (Ss might wish to discuss whether it is more logical to mention the location or the history of the Festival of Ceramics first.) The writer then mentions the selection process relating to exhibitors. The letter finishes by telling the reader what action to take if he/she is interested in exhibiting.*
>
> ***Supporting ideas***
> *In Paragraph 3 the fourth sentence (The exhibition has been ...) provides support for the first sentence (Now in its twenty-third year, the Festival of Ceramics remains the largest ...).*
>
> ***Linking words***
> *In addition (Para. 4)*
> *Therefore (Para. 5)*

9 **Ex ❺**: T asks Ss to read the example sentence and explain why the present simple has been used. Ss then look through the letter to find further examples of the present simple referring to future time. (See the end of this unit for further information on the present simple referring to future time.)

> **Conditional clauses**
>
> If these are the people you **need** ... (Para. 3)
> If you **require** ... (Para. 6)
>
> **Time clauses**
>
> by the time this letter **reaches** you ... (Para. 5)

10 T asks Ss to think of further words or phrases which are used with the present simple to refer to future time.

> **Suggested answer:**
> when, as soon as, until, after, before

11 **Ex ❻**: Ss complete the **Don't forget!** section with phrases from the letter.

> **Referring to an earlier letter or conversation:** Thank you for your interest ...
> **Enclosing:** I enclose ...
> **Offering assistance:** If you require any further information or advice, please do not hesitate to call ...
> **Referring to future contact:** I look forward to hearing from you.

12 **Ex ❼**: T introduces Ss to Writing Test Part Two (Letter). T may wish to ask Ss to prepare a detailed plan in class showing how they intend to organise their ideas before they write a letter for homework. T may also wish to refer Ss back to the points about letter writing in **Ex ❹** and **Ex ❻** at this stage.

If Ss do the writing task in class, T may wish to ask Ss to exchange their letters in pairs and give each other feedback using the **Writing Test Assessment Sheet** on page 78 of the Student's Book. Before the lesson, T should have made photocopies of the Assessment Sheet for Ss to use. (See the end of this unit for a sample letter.)

> (!) T should ensure that the Assessment Sheet has been presented clearly to Ss. (See T's notes for the **How to succeed** section of **Exam focus: Writing** for further information.)

Exam focus: Writing Test Part Two (Letter)

For Writing Test Part Two, candidates write a 200–250 word proposal, piece of business correspondence or report. All the points in the rubric must be included in the answer. To generate the range of language required at this level, the task input is broad and non-specific, which means that a reasonably high background knowledge is needed by the candidate. To ensure that no candidate is disadvantaged a choice of tasks is given. The task tests the ability to produce an appropriate piece of extended directed writing.

For the letter, candidates are expected to plan, organise and present their ideas clearly. Letters should be divided into clear paragraphs. Although candidates should not write addresses, they are expected to know letter layout and conventions, including appropriate salutations and closures. Typical written functional phrases should be used.

---

13 **Ex ❽**: Once again, the Optional Task is designed to link the lesson with the outside world. Ss use the internet or other sources to research a relevant trade fair. Ss then write a report recommending why their company should exhibit there.

Organisation of letters

Standard letter phrases

In addition to knowing letter layout and standard openings/endings (e.g. *Dear Mr Brown, Yours sincerely*), Ss need to know standard letter phrases such as:

- **Referring to previous correspondence:**
  Thank you for your interest ...
  Further to your letter of ... in which you ...
  As requested, ...

- **Stating the purpose of your letter:**
  I am writing to ...
  I would like to ...

- **Enclosing information:**
  I enclose ...
  Please find enclosed ...

- **Ending the letter:**
  If you require any further information ... do not hesitate to ...
  I look forward to hearing from you.

Main points and supporting ideas

Main points need to be clear. As a general principle, writers need to provide ideas to support and illustrate their main points.

Linking words

The relationship between ideas in a letter can be made clear through the use of linking words and phrases (showing relationships such as contrast, consequence and addition).

Present simple referring to future time

The uses of the present simple referring to future time which appear in the text are as follows.

- **In conditional clauses:**
  *If these are the people you **need** ..., you will not be disappointed.*

- **In time clauses:**
  ***By the time** this letter **reaches** you, many of the available stands will already have been rebooked.*

The present simple is used to refer to the future in subordinate clauses; the verb in the main clause usually provides the time reference. This is the case in conditionals and with the following conjunctions of time: **when**, **as soon as**, **until**, **after**, **before**, **by the time.**

The present simple can also be used to refer to future events which are considered to be certain because they are timetabled or fixed, e.g. *We **launch** the product in Europe **next week.***

Replying to an enquiry Ex ❼:

Sample answer: (219 words)

Dear Mr Zampieri

With reference to your letter dated 14 June, in which you requested information about A Cut Above, please find enclosed details about our company and the services we offer.

Our aim is always to provide our clients with the best possible combination of food, entertainment and location. By choosing A Cut Above, you can relax and enjoy your special occasion while we do all the work. Events catered for by A Cut Above include corporate functions such as conventions and Christmas balls and also family celebrations such as birthdays, weddings and anniversaries.

A Cut Above offers a variety of services from simply providing a gourmet menu to helping you choose the right venue and organise entertainment. We specialise in using our experience to meet your needs. To help us achieve this aim, we always arrange a meeting with a new client well before the date of any event in order to discuss the various possibilities.

As you can appreciate, we are unable to give quotations before our initial briefing with a client as price per head varies with choice of menu.

To arrange a meeting or for any further information, please do not hesitate to contact myself or Elena Polidoro on 01623 713698.

A Cut Above looks forward to hearing from you.

Yours sincerely

Sinead Walsh

Unit 3b Entering a market

Objectives:	To enable Ss to talk about doing business abroad
	To practise reading and listening for specific information
	To practise giving a short talk
	To practise letter writing
	To review articles

Unit overview

- **Researching a market**

Speaking	Ss discuss what aspects of a country they would research before entering a foreign market.
Reading	Ss read a bulletin on doing business in China and identify where it is from/who it is aimed at. Ss then answer comprehension questions.
Language	Ss focus on articles.
Speaking	Ss prepare and give a one-minute talk (*Speaking Test Part Two*).

- **Business practices in China**

Listening	Ss listen to a talk about doing business in China and complete notes (*Listening Test Part One*).
Speaking	Ss discuss what advice they would give to Chinese business people visiting their country.
Writing	Ss read a letter from a business acquaintance and write a letter of reply (*Writing Test Part Two*).
Optional task	Ss research a destination and prepare a brief presentation.

Researching a market

1 **Warmer (books closed):** T asks Ss what countries their company does business with. T elicits any problems associated with doing business with overseas companies or offices.

2 **Ex ❶:** T elicits what research Ss would do before entering a foreign market.

> *Suggested answer:*
> *Research into the demand for the product, market conditions, currency exchange rates, import/export mechanisms or tariffs, ways of doing business (e.g. through agents), etiquette in that culture, cultural differences*

3 **Ex ❷:** Ss read the text. T elicits where they think it is from and who they think it is aimed at.

> *The text is from a UK business magazine.*
> *The text is aimed at British companies considering doing business with China.*

4 **Ex ❸:** T asks Ss to read through the questions. Ss then read the text again to find the answers.

> *1 UK exports and imports with China are growing steadily.*
> *2 Financial services, electrical and mechanical equipment, aviation and environmental technology and vehicles.*
> *3 Ignorance of the cultural differences between the Western and Eastern ways of doing business.*
> *4 Long term commitment, building relationships with prospective Chinese partners, earning respect.*
> *5 To find a Chinese colleague to help in negotiations. Also a visit by a foreigner is seen as an indication of commitment and sincerity.*

5 **Ex ❹:** T asks Ss to read through the text and highlight any articles (*a, an, the*). T then asks Ss to comment on the main differences in use between English and their own language. Ss also need to consider differences relating to the omission of articles (zero article). (See the end of this unit for further information on articles.)

6   **Ex ❺:** T introduces Ss to Speaking Test Part Two. T stresses the importance of having a maximum of three main points and supporting and illustrating these main points briefly. T also encourages Ss to think of an opening and closing sentence for their talk. T may wish to refer Ss to the framework for planning short talks on page 81 of the Student's Book. Ss take turns to make and listen to each other's short talks. Those listening should be encouraged to make notes and ask questions at the end. T may wish to ask Ss to use the Short Talk section of the **Speaking Test Assessment Sheet** on page 83 of the Student's Book to evaluate each other's performance. Before the lesson, T should have made photocopies of the Assessment Sheet for Ss to use.

(!)   T should ensure that the Assessment Sheet has been presented clearly to Ss. (See T's notes for the **How to succeed** section of **Exam focus: Speaking** for further information.)

(!)   The **Exam focus audio CD** contains recordings of model answers of most of the Short Talk tasks in the book. However, as this is the first time Ss have been introduced to Speaking Test Part Two, no recordings are provided.

Exam focus: Speaking Test Part Two

Each candidate chooses a topic from a list of three options (one general, one general business and one specialised business topic) and speaks about it for one minute. To avoid overlap, the candidates receive different lists. When each candidate has finished speaking, the other candidate has an opportunity to ask one or two questions. Candidates can take notes during their partner's presentations.

Candidates have one minute to think about what they want to say and should use the time to make notes. Ss are expected to plan, organise and present their ideas clearly. They should use appropriate phrases to structure their talk.

This exercise differs from the exam in that here there are only two topics to choose from. In the exam itself candidates choose from three options.

Business practices in China

7   **Ex ❶:** This exercise practises the skills needed for Listening Test Part One. T asks Ss to read through the notes and predict what sort of information or word types could be used to complete each sentence. Ss listen and complete the notes.

   These answers are bolded in T's audioscript.

1 *standards and expectations*	2 *preparatory work*	3 *late (for meetings)*
4 *congestion*	5 *senior manager*	6 *business cards*
7 *brief introduction*	8 *audio-visual aids*	9 *(special) dinner*
10 *children*	11 *hospitality*	12 *(sightseeing)(trips)*

Exam focus: Listening Test Part One

Candidates listen to a monologue (or a series of long turns by more than one speaker) and complete each of the gaps in the text with up to three words or a number. There are twelve gaps in total. The recording is heard twice. This task tests the ability to listen for and note specific information.

Candidates have 45 seconds to read through the input before listening and should use the time to think about what might fit in the gaps. The questions follow the order of the recording. Candidates are expected to write the **exact words** used in the recording. Provided that the words written are recognisable, candidates are not penalised for incorrect spelling.

---

8 **Ex ❷**: Ss discuss what advice they would give Chinese people visiting their country. If Ss are unsure about what kind of advice to give, T encourages them to consider the same type of situations as in Ex ❶ and to think about the differences between Chinese behaviour and their own.

9 **Ex ❸**: The exercise practises the skills needed for Writing Test Part Two (Letter). T may wish to ask Ss to prepare a detailed plan in class showing how they intend to organise their ideas before they write a letter for homework. When setting the task, T may wish to refer Ss back to Unit 3a for useful letter phrases.

If Ss do the writing task in class, T may wish to ask Ss to exchange letters in pairs and give each other feedback using the **Writing Test Assessment Sheet** on page 78 of the Student's Book. Before the lesson, T should have made photocopies of the Assessment Sheet for Ss to use. (See the end of this unit for a sample letter.)

(!) T should ensure that the Assessment Sheet has been presented clearly to Ss. (See T's notes for the **How to succeed** section of **Exam focus: Writing** for further information.)

Exam focus: Writing Test Part Two (Letter)

For Writing Test Part Two, candidates write a 200–250 word proposal, piece of business correspondence or report. All the points in the rubric must be included in the answer. To generate the range of language required at this level, the task input is broad and non-specific, which means that a reasonably high background knowledge is needed by the candidate. To ensure that no candidate is disadvantaged a choice of tasks is given. The task tests the ability to produce an appropriate piece of extended directed writing.

For the letter, candidates are expected to plan, organise and present their ideas clearly. Letters should be divided into clear paragraphs. Although candidates should not write addresses, they are expected to know letter layout and conventions, including appropriate salutations and closures. Typical written functional phrases should be used.

---

10 **Ex ❹**: Once again, the Optional Task is designed to link the lesson with the outside world. Ss research a destination and prepare a brief presentation to be delivered in the next lesson. T should stress the need for organisation and for Ss to consider how best to hold the interest of the audience. T may wish to ask Ss to consider which of the locations presented they would most like to visit and why.

Articles

The uses of the indefinite, definite and zero article which appear in the text are as follows.

Indefinite article (*a/an*)

- **When something is unspecific – one of many, precisely which one is not important:**
  *However there are **a** number of strategies for working with the Chinese ...*
- **When something is mentioned for the first time, before a shared context has been established:**
  *The Olympics in 2008 provided **a** valuable bridge between Beijing and London, ...*

Definite article (*the*)

- **When the reference to something is clear because it is the only one:**
  *With one of **the** world's fastest rates of ...*
- **When the reference to something is clear because it is defined:**
  *Success in China will require ... **the** ability to research the market.*
- **When the reference to something is clear because a shared context has already been established:**
  *It will almost always be necessary to visit **the** market ...*
- **When referring to superlatives:**
  *... partner is vital for **the** most successful commercial transactions.*
- **When referring to a nationality:**
  *... for working with **the** Chinese and it is vital to recognise ....*
- **When the name of a country is plural or is made up of an adjective and a general noun:**
  *Now in 2011 **the** UK is continuing to encourage ...*
- **When referring to a region within a country:**
  *... a great deal in China, initially in **the** south, but now throughout the country.*

No article is used

- **With most country names:**
  Although imports from China ...
- **With uncountable nouns referring to a general concept:**
  ***Success** in China will require long term **commitment**.*
- **When referring to general plural nouns:**
  Virtually all transactions in China result from ...
- **When referring to general plural or uncountable nouns qualified by an adjective:**
  *With one of the world's fastest rates of **economic growth** and a population ...*

T may wish to remind Ss that, as a basic rule, a singular countable noun cannot stand alone in English but needs to be preceded by a determiner: *my, his, that, next, a, the, some*. T may also wish to remind Ss that an uncountable noun never takes *a/an*.

Ss should also be aware that nouns followed by *of* are often preceded by *the*: *... **the** main source **of** ...*

Business practices in China Ex ❸:

Sample answer: *(244 words)*

Dear Chen

I was very pleased to receive your letter. As requested, I enclose some advice about visiting Milan.

There are lots of good hotels near the Fiera and I recommend the Hotel Wagner; it is about a ten-minute walk from the trade fair but also has metro and tram connections. The public transport system here is quite reliable and I do not think you need to hire a car; the traffic in Milan can be a bit chaotic.

Finding somewhere to eat in the evening should be easy. There are plenty of restaurants and pizzerias near the hotel. My favourite is Nove Cento, which serves excellent seafood pasta.

It is difficult to know what to recommend for sightseeing as the city has so much to offer. If you are interested in art, then the world famous 'Last Supper' by Leonardo da Vinci is a short tram ride from the hotel or you could visit the Brera art gallery. There is also the Duomo, Milan's huge gothic cathedral. If you are interested in football, there should be a midweek match featuring either AC or Inter Milan. Alternatively, you could visit the fashion area around via Montenapoleone.

Thank you for inviting me for a meal one evening during your stay. I would be very happy to accept.

I look forward to hearing from you nearer the time. We can then make arrangements for where and when we are going to meet.

Best regards

Maurizio

Unit 4a The future of work

Objectives:	To enable Ss to talk about changes in working practices
	To practise reading and listening for specific information
	To review the language of predictions

Unit overview

- ### Visions

Reading 1	Ss read an extract about work in the future and discuss the issues involved.

- ### Predictions

Reading 2	Ss read five predictions about the future and match the statements with the predictions (*Reading Test Part One*).
Language	Ss focus on the language of predictions.
Speaking	Ss discuss the statements and say whether they agree with them.

- ### Reality

Listening	Ss listen to an interview about setting up a multi-occupant office building and answer multiple-choice comprehension questions (*Listening Test Part Three*).
Speaking	Ss discuss several statements on working practices and consider the merits of each one.
Optional task	Ss use the internet to find out more about shared office space and prepare a summary about the pros and cons of office sharing.

Visions

1   **Warmer (books closed):** T asks Ss about changes that have taken place in working practices since they started their jobs. Ss should think about use of faxes, email, the internet etc.

2   **Ex ❶:** Before Ss read the extract, T asks Ss to look at the picture and elicits what the scene evokes for them. Ss then read the extract and discuss their answers to the questions.

Predictions

3   **Ex ❶:** T introduces Ss to Reading Test Part One. Ss read the texts and statements and match each statement with a text. (T should discourage Ss from giving their views on the predictions at this stage since this forms the basis of **Ex ❸**.)

1 Megan	2 Sachin	3 Joshua	4 Jeanne
5 Janice	6 Megan	7 Joshua	8 Sachin

> **Exam focus: Reading Test Part One**
>
> Candidates read a single text or five short related texts and eight statements. Ss then match each statement with the text it refers to. This tests ability to read for gist and global meaning.
>
> Candidates should check that each text has been matched with only one statement.

4   **Ex ❷:** Before Ss do the exercise, T elicits ways of predicting the future. T should be prepared to discuss differences between *will* and *going to* at this point. However, T should also widen the discussion to cover adverbs which can reinforce or weaken a prediction (e.g. *undoubtedly*) and lexical ways of talking about the future (e.g. *be set to*).

Ss then read the texts again and find ways of predicting the future. Ss order the predictions from most to least definite (grouping the predictions, rather than ordering each one separately). T reminds Ss that in spoken language the use of full forms (e.g. *will*) and contractions (e.g. *'ll*) and the use of intonation can increase or decrease the strength of a prediction. (See the end of this unit for further information on predictions.)

will definitely + verb (Megan)
'll undoubtedly + verb (Joshua)
will / 'll + verb (Jeanne, Janice, Sachin)
is certainly going to + verb (Megan)
are going to + verb (Janice)
is set to + verb (Janice)
're bound to + verb (Joshua)

's likely to + verb (Jeanne)
will probably + verb (Jeanne)

may + verb (Megan)

5 **Ex ❸:** Ss discuss briefly which of the statements they agree with.

> **Supplementary activity**
>
> If there is time, T asks Ss to write a couple of sentences about the future of work on pieces of paper. (T encourages Ss to vary the language they use in their predictions.) T collects the papers and reads them out to the class. Ss try to guess who wrote each comment.

Reality

6 **Ex ❶:** This exercise practises the skills needed for Listening Test Part Three. T asks Ss to read through the questions before listening. When checking the answers, T may wish to ask Ss to identify where the answers appeared in the audioscript.

1 C	2 A	3 B	4 A
5 B	6 A	7 B	8 C

> **Exam focus: Listening Test Part Three**
>
> Candidates listen to a 3–4 minute recording of two or three speakers and answer eight multiple-choice questions. The recording is heard twice. This task tests ability to listen for specific information.
>
> The questions follow the order of the recording and are clearly signposted by the speaker(s). Incorrect options are included in the recording in order to distract unwary candidates.

7 T asks Ss if they think sharing an office space is a good idea for people who are self-employed and often work alone.

8 **Ex ❷:** Ss work in pairs to discuss the three statements about working practices. Encourage them to think about the merits of each statement, even if they do not necessarily agree with it. Ss then decide how they would change each statement to reflect good working practices.

9 **Ex ❸:** Once again, the Optional Task is designed to link the lesson with the outside world. Ss use the internet to find other examples of shared office space users. Explain they need to think about the pros and cons of sharing and organise their summary accordingly.

Predictions

T may like to point out the basic difference between *going to* and *will* to talk about predictions.

The essential factor in the use of *going to* for predictions is a focus on some present factor which the speaker feels certain will lead to a future event. In other words, the speaker feels that he/she has evidence of what is about to happen.

e.g. *With the growth in teleworking, how **are** authorities **going to** cope ...?*

As with any modal, *will* refers to the speaker's judgement of the situation. In other words, *will* is used to make predictions about things we know or expect will happen based on past experience or intuition.

e.g. *Part-time staff may be working for one employer in the morning and a different one in the afternoon, so values and branding **will** need to be stronger.*

It is often possible to use *going to* and *will* for predictions virtually interchangeably; the use may vary according to the speaker. However, *will* is commonly used for predictions in formal writing.

The strength of a prediction can be shown by the use of qualifiers such as *probably* and *undoubtedly*.

e.g. *Working hours will **probably** change quite dramatically.*
*There'll **undoubtedly** be companies realising the importance of their social obligations.*

In addition to using *will* and *going to* to make predictions, Ss should think about ways of expressing the future lexically.

e.g. *The distinction between the employed and self-employed **is set to** disappear.*
*We **are bound to** see a move towards promoting lifestyle issues in the office.*

Unit 4b e-business

Objectives:	To enable Ss to talk about e-business
	To practise reading for specific information
	To practise listening for gist and specific information
	To practise describing trends in writing
	To review the future perfect and future continuous

Unit overview

- ### What is e-business?

Speaking	Ss discuss how they use the internet at work.
Reading	Ss look at a page from a website about e-business and identify the difference between e-business, e-commerce and e-marketing and the benefits of each.
Speaking	Ss discuss what difficulties might be experienced with e-business and e-commerce.

- ### The advantages of e-business

Listening	Ss listen to five people talk about how e-business has transformed their companies and decide which areas of business have been transformed and the benefits (*Listening Test Part Two*).
Language	Ss focus on the future perfect and future continuous.
Writing	Ss write a description of a graph comparing the predicted growth in online retail sales and in-store sales influenced by websites (*Writing Test Part One*).
Optional task	Ss research and write a report about a company's website.

What is e-business?

This unit focuses on e-business and e-commerce. The term *e-commerce* (also known as *e-trading*) is connected with retailing and describes company to consumer communication using the internet, e.g. when a customer orders and pays for books over the internet. The term *e-business* is broader, referring to the transformation of fundamental business processes through the use of internet technologies. It refers to the way internal business processes and communication with suppliers etc. are carried out via computer networks that use web-compatible software.

1 **Ex ❶:** Ss briefly discuss how they use the internet at work and how their business uses the internet differently from ten years ago.

2 **Ex ❷:** Ask Ss to look at the B2B logo at the bottom of the page and make suggestions about what this organisation might do (provides independent digital business consultancy, training and research).

3 **Ex ❸:** Ss read the page from the website and write a definition of e-business, e-trading, e-support and e-marketing.

> *Suggested answer:*
> *e-business: term used to describe the information systems and applications that support and drive business processes, most often using web technologies.*
>
> *e-trading (also known as e-commerce): term used to describe the selling of goods and services online.*
>
> *e-support: term used to describe the online technologies available to support a company's customers*
>
> *e-marketing: the use of the internet and related technologies to achieve marketing goals. Often revolves round a company's website.*

4 **Ex ❹:** Ss discuss the benefits of e-business, e-trading, e-support and e-marketing.

> *Suggested answer:*
> *e-business: The technology is simple, low cost or free. It can improve product promotion both internally and externally and increase sales by using e-commerce technologies. Integrated office systems improve the effectiveness of business processes and can reduce communication and travel costs. Systems also help improve relations between supplier and customer by keeping track of interactions.*
>
> *e-trading: Can support growth of a businesses' revenue by attracting new customers in all markets by using an online sales channel. Can reduce costs and improve efficiency through automation and by creating a low-cost route to market for products. Internet sales offer a higher margin than traditional routes.*
>
> *e-support: Low cost online technologies support customers, providing information about products and services on a company's website.*
>
> *e-marketing: When integrated with traditional marketing strategies, online marketing can be very effective. Costs are lower, wider audiences can be reached and campaigns can be targeted and interactive.*

5 When Ss have thought about the benefits of e-business ask them to suggest some of the possible problems which might be experienced with e-business and e-commerce. T may wish to divide Ss into pairs or small groups and ask some Ss to think about potential difficulties for companies and others to think about difficulties for customers.

>
> *Suggested answer:*
> **Possible difficulties for companies:** *cost of installing systems and training staff, need to provide 24-hour service/back-up, keeping up-to-date with technical advances, potential systems failures (viruses/Millennium bug)*
>
> **Possible difficulties for customers:** *need to have up-to-date, reliable internet access (for e-commerce customers), lack of confidence in system security*

The advantages of e-business

6 **Ex ❶:** This exercise practises the skills needed in Listening Test Part Two. Ss listen to a set of five extracts twice and complete two tasks for each extract. T points out that for the first extract Ss should answer questions 1 and 6, for the second extract 2 and 7 etc. T asks Ss to read through the lists of business areas and benefits and think of words or phrases they would expect to hear connected with each one. For example, for *training methods*, Ss might expect to hear words such as *teacher, trainer, seminar*. Ss then listen and match each speaker with a business area and benefit. (After Ss have completed the task, T may wish to point out that the exam texts are unlikely to contain as much technical vocabulary and should therefore be less difficult.)

1 H	*2 G*	*3 C*	*4 D*	*5 F*
6 J	*7 I*	*8 O*	*9 M*	*10 N*

> **Exam focus: Listening Test Part Two**
>
> Candidates listen to five short topic-related extracts and complete two tasks, which may involve identifying any combination of the following for each extract: speaker, topic, function, opinion or feelings. The five extracts are heard twice. Both tasks test candidates' ability to listen for gist and specific information.
>
> Candidates should be aware that each extract contains both a Task One answer and a Task Two answer. Some candidates may prefer to deal with Task One during the first listening and Task Two during the second listening, or they may choose to attempt the two tasks simultaneously. For each task, they have a list of eight options to choose from. Incorrect options are included in the recordings in order to distract unwary candidates.

7 **Ex ❷:** T refers Ss to the example sentences. Ss then look through the audioscript to find further examples of the future perfect and future continuous and discuss how they are used. Ss then discuss whether other future forms could be used with the same effect. (See the end of this unit for further information on the future perfect and future continuous.)

> *Future perfect and future continuous forms are bolded in T's audioscript.*
>
> *No alternative verb forms are possible where the future perfect is used.*
>
> *However, alternatives for the future continuous are possible: **will, going to** and the present continuous could all be used, with differences in meaning. No other wording would need to be changed; however, the nuances conveyed by the future continuous would be lost.*

8 **Ex ❸:** This exercise practises the skills needed in Writing Test Part One. The text above the graph is for interest only; T may wish to use it as the basis for discussion but Ss do not have to take it into account in their answers. T checks that Ss understand that *business to business* on the graph refers to e-business; *business to consumer* refers to e-commerce.

When setting up this task, T may wish to refer Ss back to Unit 2a for the language of trends and Unit 4a for the language of predictions. T may wish to ask Ss to compare e-business and e-commerce orally in class before they write a report for homework. If Ss do the writing task in class, T may wish to ask Ss to exchange reports in pairs and give each other feedback.

> *Suggested answer:*   *(140 words)*
> *Since 2009 companies have been looking to the internet to increase their market share by accessing the increasing number of consumers using the internet. The influence of the web has been reflected in the continuous growth of sales in the US retail trade, with revenue rising consistently each year.*
>
> *Retail sales influenced by the web, as well as direct online sales, have been steadily increasing over the years and this trend looks set to continue. From $1,072 billion in 2009 experts predict that web-influenced sales will have reached $1,409 billion by 2014 and direct online sales will have risen to $249 billion, up from $155 billion five years earlier. In addition the percentage growth of these sales compared with total retail sales has grown from 42% to 48% in 2011 and is expected to rise further to 53% by 2014.*

Exam focus: Writing Test Part One

Candidates write a 120–140 word report describing trends. The task tests concise writing skills.

Candidates are expected to describe, compare and contrast information presented visually, in the form of graphs, bar charts and pie charts. Candidates should use appropriate language of trends and must be concise in order to avoid exceeding the strict word limit.

This exercise differs from the exam in that Ss are also expected to refer to future trends in this case. In the exam itself, Ss are likely to be asked to report past trends.

---

9 **Ex ❹:** Once again, the aim of the Optional Task is to link the lesson with the outside world. Ss research and write a report on a website. Although Ss are free to choose any website to write a report on, Ss should be encouraged to use their own company's site if there is one. T reminds Ss to consider the features of good reports in their answers.

Future perfect and future continuous

The uses of the future perfect and future continuous which appear in the audioscript are as follows.

Future perfect

- **To refer to actions completed by a certain time in the future:**
  By the end of the year we'll have reduced our paper invoices from five million to zero.

In phrases which contain a reference to actions completed by a specific time in the future, the future perfect cannot be substituted by other future forms.

Future continuous

- **To refer to actions which are arranged or expected to happen:**
  We'll be introducing more and more new product lines.

The future continuous can also be used to refer to an action which is in progress at a certain time in the future.
e.g.   *We'll already be discussing the launch by the time you get there.*

The future continuous can also be used as a polite form, when making enquiries about a person's future plans.
e.g.   *Will you be staying for the reception?*

It is not possible to replace the future continuous with other verb forms when it is used to refer to an action in progress at a certain time in the future. However, when the future continuous is used to refer to something which is expected/a matter of course in the future, or when it is used as a polite form, alternatives are possible – though always resulting in a change in emphasis.

e.g.   *We'll be introducing more new product lines*   This is what we're doing anyway.
        We're going to introduce more new product lines   This is our intention.
        We're introducing more new product lines   This is our specific plan.

        Will you be staying for the reception?   May I ask if you intend to stay?
        Are you staying for the reception?   I'd like to know if you are staying.

Exam focus

Objectives:	To familiarise Ss with the content of the Reading, Listening, Writing and Speaking Tests
	To provide useful exam tips

Section overview

- **The Reading Test**

  T provides an overview of the Reading Test and some tips on how to succeed. T then takes Ss through each part of the Reading Test: Ss do an exam-related activity for each part. T provides exam tips and warns Ss against typical traps they might fall into.

- **The Listening Test**

  T provides an overview of the Listening Test. T then divides tips on how to succeed into *Before listening, While listening* and *After listening*.

- **The Writing Test** (Materials needed: Sufficient copies of **Writing Test Assessment Sheet**)

  T provides an overview of the Writing Test and some tips on how to succeed. Ss then focus on Part One and assess how well a sample answer fulfils the task set before rewriting the sample answer more concisely. Ss then assess a sample answer for a Part Two report-writing task and summarise the writer's main points and supporting ideas. Ss focus on the organisation of reports then rewrite the sample answer. Finally, Ss do a Part Two letter-writing task based on preparatory notes. Before writing, Ss focus on how to plan formal letters.

- **The Speaking Test** (Materials needed: Sufficient copies of **Speaking Test Assessment Sheet**, one set of **twelve cards** per group to be photocopied, *Pass Cambridge BEC Higher* Exam focus audio CD)

  T provides an overview of the Speaking Test and some tips on how to succeed. The rest of this section takes Ss through all three parts of the Speaking Test: Part One (Personal Information), Part Two (Short Talk) and Part Three (Collaborative Task). To support this process, T plays relevant parts of a mock Speaking Test in which the candidates do a bad followed by a good version of Part Two and Part Three. Ss also have a chance to practise for the exam themselves. In addition, Ss can listen to model answers of the short talks in Part Two.

The Reading Test: Overview

1 **Warmer (books closed):** T asks Ss what they know about the Reading Test (type of tasks, length etc.). Ss then open their books and read through the overview. T explains the key features of the Reading Test and answers any questions Ss may have questions about the format and administration of the exam.

2 T may wish to show Ss an example of a *Cambridge ESOL BEC Higher Sample/Past Paper* in order to clarify the format and requirements of the exam. T need not focus at this stage on how to approach each part of the exam; this will be done later in this unit.

3 T points out that the Reading and Writing Tests are combined in one exam paper lasting 130 minutes. T suggests that Ss should complete the Reading Test and transfer their answers within 60 minutes, leaving 70 minutes for the Writing Test.

4 T tells Ss that they may write on their Question Papers, but answers must be transferred to the Answer Sheets in **pencil**. T may wish to show an example of an Answer Sheet at this stage. T explains that no extra time is allowed for transferring answers so Ss should plan their time carefully. A warning that the exam is reaching its end will be given five minutes before the official finishing time.

How to succeed

5 T quickly brainstorms good advice for doing the Reading Test (read the instructions carefully etc.). T then takes Ss through the tips listed and explains them in further detail.

The reading tasks

6 T tells Ss they will now work through short exercises dealing with each part of the Reading Test and providing techniques for dealing with each task. T may wish to show Ss an example of each part of the exam from a past paper when working through the exercises. T may also wish to point out at this stage that Ss have the opportunity of doing full practice tests using *Cambridge ESOL BEC Higher Sample/Past Papers.*

7 **Ex ❶:** T points out the format and aim of Part One of the Reading Test and refers Ss to the **Exam tips**. Ss read the three sentences and match one sentence with the text. In feedback, Ss discuss which parts of the text helped them choose their answer. Ss also discuss how and why an unwary candidate might be tempted to choose the wrong answer (e.g. *not technical know-how*).

 *Sentence 3 is correct. The relevant part of the text is: **More than 100 case studies ... successfully exploited.** (line 7)*

Exam focus: Reading Test Part One

Candidates read a single text or five short related texts and eight statements. Ss then match each statement with the text it refers to. This tests ability to read for gist and global meaning.

Candidates should check that each text has been matched with only one statement.

---

8 **Ex ❷:** T points out the format and aim of Part Two of the Reading Test and refers Ss to the **Exam tips**. Ss read the text and insert one of the three sentences into the gap. In feedback, T elicits the reasons why the remaining sentences do not fit.

> *Sentence B is correct. The answer depends on the sentence following the gap: **This might not be cheap** ... The correct sentence needs to refer to something which could be expensive.*

Exam focus: Reading Test Part Two

Candidates read a 450–500 word text and complete the six gaps from a choice of eight sentences. Sentence H is the example sentence and one other sentence is a distractor and does not fit any of the gaps. This tests the ability to read for detail and understand cohesion and text structure.

Candidates read the whole text for general understanding and then the options. They re-read the text and fill any gaps they feel sure of, always reading before and after a gap to ensure a sentence fits appropriately. They then concentrate on any remaining gaps. Finally, they read their completed text, checking overall coherence, grammatical agreement and cohesive devices such as linking words (e.g. *however*) and reference words (e.g. *this*).

---

9 **Ex ❸:** T points out the format and aim of Part Three of the Reading Test and refers Ss to the **Exam tips**. Ss then read the paragraph and choose one of the options to answer the question. In feedback, Ss discuss which parts of the text helped them choose their answer. Ss also discuss which words in the paragraph might suggest the incorrect options (e.g. *freefone product information hotlines, telephone-based distribution networks*).

> *C is correct. The relevant part of the text is: ... **consumers now expect quick access to information** ...*

Exam focus: Reading Test Part Three

Candidates read a 50–600 word text and answer six multiple-choice questions. This tests ability to read for specific information.

Candidates read the whole text briefly for general understanding and then read the questions and options. Ss re-read the text and answer the questions they feel sure of. They then concentrate on scanning the text for the answers to the remaining questions. The questions follow the order of the text, which should help Ss narrow down the location of a relevant passage in the text.

---

10 Ex ❹: T points out the format and aim of Part Four of the Reading Test and refers Ss to the **Exam tips**. Ss read through the text and underline the words around each gap which indicate the type of word missing which will help them choose the correct option. Ss then think of possible words for each gap.

Suggested answer:
1   **is of ... to**
    positive noun, e.g. value, interest, benefit, importance
2   **high-calibre, ... staff**
    positive adjective, e.g. professional, valued, motivated, well-trained
3   **a ... of able people**
    collective noun, e.g. team, group, body, number
4   **management positions which inevitably ...**
    verb which collocates with position, e.g. come up, arise
5   **opportunity to ... their careers**
    positive verb which collocates with careers, e.g. further, develop, advance
6   **to help them ... effectively**
    verb, e.g. work, operate, perform
7   **to assist us in ... your development**
    gerund which collocates with development, e.g. monitoring, checking, evaluating
8   **This booklet ... It also ... appraisal procedures**
    verb which collocates with procedures, e.g. lists, outlines, explains
9   **you ... your records up to date**
    verb which collocates with records and up to date, e.g. keep
10 **be able to ... your future development needs**
    verb which collocates with future needs, e.g. predict, estimate, outline, plan, project

---

Exam focus: Reading Test Part Four

Candidates read a single business-related text of approximately 250 words and choose the correct word for each of the ten gaps from a set of four options (e.g. *commission, contract, agreement, arrangement*). This tests vocabulary.

---

11 Ex ❺: Ss complete each of the gaps with one of the multiple-choice options. T may wish to ask Ss to discuss the precise meanings of the remaining options and in what contexts they would be possible.

1 C	2 A	3 B	4 B	5 C
6 A	7 D	8 A	9 B	10 C

12 Ex ❻: T points out the format and aim of Part Five of the Reading Test and refers Ss to the **Exam tips**. T reminds Ss to pay particular attention to the use of features such as relative pronouns, comparatives, auxiliary verbs and conjunctions. Ss read the text and underline the words around each gap which help them identify the missing word. Ss then complete each of the gaps with one word.

1	less	2	that	3	despite	4	however	5	no
6	such	7	which	8	between	9	while/whilst/whereas	10	rather

> **Exam focus: Reading Test Part Five**
>
> Candidates read a business-related text of approximately 250 words and complete each of the ten gaps with a suitable word. This tests understanding of the items which produce a coherent and cohesive text, with particular emphasis on grammar.

13 Ex ❼: T points out the format and aim of Part Six of the Reading Test and refers Ss to the **Exam tips**. Ss then read the text and decide whether each line is correct or contains an extra word. In feedback, Ss discuss which sentences are incorrect and why.

1	Correct	2	every	3	they	4	order	5	Correct
6	a	7	Correct	8	which	9	Correct	10	the

> **Exam Focus: Reading Test Part Six**
>
> Candidates read a short text of approximately 150–200 words containing twelve numbered lines and decide whether each line is correct or contains an extra word (e.g. a superfluous article or auxiliary). This tests ability to proofread. Candidates are expected to write CORRECT if a line is correct.

The Listening Test: Overview

1 Warmer (books closed): T asks Ss what they know about the Listening Test (type of tasks, length etc.). Ss then open their books and read through the overview.

2 T takes Ss briefly through the three parts of the test to ensure Ss understand the requirements of each. T points out that Ss have to listen for gist and specific information and complete gap-fill, matching and multiple-choice exercises. T may wish to show Ss at this stage an example of a *Cambridge ESOL BEC Higher Sample/Past Paper* in order to clarify the format and requirements of the Listening Test.

T tells Ss that they may write on their Question Papers, but answers must be transferred to the Answer Sheets in **pencil**. T may wish to show an example of an Answer Sheet at this stage. T explains that Ss are allowed ten minutes to transfer their answers at the end of the exam.

Listening Test Part One: Candidates listen to a monologue (or a series of long turns by more than one speaker) and complete each gap in the text with up to three words or a number. There are twelve gaps in total. The recording is heard twice. This task tests ability to listen for and note specific information. Candidates are expected to write the **exact words** used in the recording.

Listening Test Part Two: Candidates listen to five short topic-related extracts and complete two tasks, which may involve identifying any combination of the following for each extract: speaker, topic, function, opinion or feelings. The five extracts are heard twice. Candidates should be aware that each extract contains both a Task One answer and a Task Two answer. Both tasks test candidates' ability to listen for gist and specific information.

Listening Test Part Three: Candidates listen to a 3–4 minute recording of two or three speakers and answer eight multiple-choice questions. The recording is heard twice. This task tests ability to listen for specific information.

Before listening

3 Books closed: T writes the headings *Before listening, While listening* and *After listening* on the board. Ss brainstorm advice for candidates under these headings. In the rest of the lesson T will work through advice and activities related to these stages. At the end of the lesson T can compare the advice given in the book with what the Ss brainstormed.

4 Ss open their books. T takes them through the tips for pre-listening.

5 Ex ❶: T reminds Ss of the importance of predicting language from what is already provided in the task. Ss then read the form and predict words to fill the gaps. T should tell Ss that although they will not hear the actual recordings on this occasion, they should use the same strategy when dealing with Part One of the Listening Test.

> ***Suggested answer:***
> *1   a welcome speech/an introductory talk*
> *2   the year's performance/the group*
> *3   coffee/refreshments*

While listening

6   T refers Ss to the **Exam tip**. T warns Ss of the danger of jumping to conclusions when listening. Distractors such as word spots or synonyms are included deliberately in order to mislead unwary candidates.

7   **Ex ❶:** Ss read the question and the extract from the audioscript and choose the correct option. Ss then discuss why some candidates might have chosen the wrong option.

> *The correct answer is **B**. The relevant part of the text is: ... **in the end we decided to revamp our lines ... fresh exciting ideas.***
>
> *Some candidates might be misled by the phrase **cutting production costs** and choose A. However, the speaker says that this idea was only considered, rather than carried out.*
>
> *Other candidates might choose C because the speaker refers to **aggressive discounting**. However, the speaker says they felt winning back customers with new ideas would be a better idea.*

⚠   T should also point out at this stage that the questions in Part Three follow the order of the recording. Each question is clearly signposted by the speaker(s), often by using words from the actual question to indicate that it is due to be answered.

After listening

8   **Ex ❶:** T reminds Ss of the importance of checking their answers carefully. Ss then find the mistakes in the sample answers.

> ***Part One:*** *In gap 1 the candidate has written more than three words. The rubric specifically states that the candidate should write up to three words or a number.*
>
> ***Part Two:*** *In gap 13 the candidate has written A/B. It is impossible to know which answer he/she means so no credit can be given. Moreover, the candidate has used A in both gaps 13 and 14.*
>
> ***Part Three:*** *The candidate has selected A and C here, even though the rubric states that only one letter should be chosen.*

9   T reminds Ss that although the answers on page 71 of the Student's Book are written on the question papers, final answers must be transferred to the Answer Sheet in the actual exam.

The Writing Test: Overview

1 **Warmer (books closed):** T asks Ss what they know about the Writing Test (type of tasks, length etc.). T puts Ss' answers on the board and asks Ss what they find most difficult about the writing tasks they have encountered in *Pass Cambridge BEC Higher* so far (e.g. keeping to the word limit).

2 Ss then open their books and read through the overview. T explains the key features of the Writing Test and answers any questions Ss may have about the requirements of each part of the test.

T reminds Ss that the Reading and Writing Tests are combined in one exam paper lasting 130 minutes. T suggests that Ss should complete the Reading Test within 60 minutes, leaving 70 minutes for the Writing Test.

Candidates are expected to write their answers on the official Answer Sheet. In addition, they will be given rough paper for notes. Candidates should use the rough paper to plan their writing. However, they should be aware that if they write the complete answers in rough first, there may not be enough time to copy out the final version.

3 T explains that in this lesson he/she will illustrate the two different parts of the Writing Test and focus on the requirements of both parts.

How to succeed

4 T asks Ss what they think the examiner is looking for in the Writing Test. Ss' responses might include: grammatical accuracy, good range of business vocabulary, organisation, use of appropriate language and spelling. T quickly brainstorms good advice (e.g. use sequencers to organise your ideas clearly, demonstrate a range of vocabulary by not repeating a word when an alternative is available).

5 Ss read through the tips regarding Task and Language and compare the tips with their suggestions. T stresses that in the exam the candidate must complete the task in full and use consistent, natural language.

T then introduces Ss to the **Writing Test Assessment Sheet** on page 78 and points out any similarities with the suggestions brainstormed by Ss earlier. T emphasises that this checklist is particularly useful for Part Two of the Writing Test and that T will use the Assessment Sheet throughout the course to provide Ss with feedback on their letter and report writing. In addition, Ss will be able to use the Assessment Sheet for self and peer evaluation purposes.

6 T refers Ss to sections of the book which will help them in the Writing Test. In addition to looking at this section of the book (**Exam focus**), Ss can refer to Unit 1a for report writing, Unit 2a for describing graphs, Unit 2b for linking words and phrases, Unit 3a for letter writing phrases and Units 5a and 7b for formal report language.

Describing graphs

7 T reminds Ss that in Part One of the Writing Test they will have to describe a graph. T elicits advice for completing this task successfully (e.g. be concise, keep to the word limit). Ss then read the **Exam tip**.

Exam focus: Writing Test Part One

Candidates write a 120–140 word report describing trends. The task tests concise writing skills.

Candidates are expected to describe, compare and contrast information presented visually, in the form of graphs, bar charts and pie charts. Candidates should use appropriate language of trends and must be concise in order to avoid exceeding the strict word limit.

---

8 **Ex ❶**: Ss work in pairs. T asks Ss to read the task and then the sample answer. Ss then discuss whether the answer fulfils the task.

Suggested answer:
The candidate only partially fulfils the task. At 195 words, the sample answer is well over the word limit. Moreover, although the candidate describes the graph, he/she does not start to compare the performance of the two companies until Para. 2.

9 **Ex ❷**: In this exercise Ss will focus on conciseness, an awareness of which is useful for both parts of the Writing Test but particularly Part One. T checks that Ss understand the terms used in the exercise. Ss consider how they affect the conciseness of the sample answer. To save time, T may wish to assign one category per pair.

In feedback, T should point out that the sample answer could be more concise if there were shorter and less wordy sentences, less repetition and redundancy and more use of features such as ellipsis and reference words. (See the end of this unit for further information on conciseness.)

T also elicits other ways in which the sample answer could be improved (an overall description of the important points rather than a detailed description of individual points, more varied trends language, use of linking words and phrases to aid the reader etc.). Ss then rewrite the answer in 120–140 words. T may wish to ask Ss to exchange their answers and give each other feedback.

Suggested answer: *(124 words)*
Although sales at both ASEF Chemicals and Chemicon Ltd experienced a number of fluctuations over the period 2005–2009, turnover at both companies showed a general upward trend.

At the beginning of the period ASEF sales stood at just over $30m. They experienced a fall the following year, before picking up again in 2007 and reaching a peak of $60m in 2008. Sales fell again slightly the following year but remained higher than their 2007 level. Chemicon sales exceeded those of ASEF in 2005 ($42m compared to $31m). Despite experiencing a fall in 2007, the overall trend was a slight rise over the four year period. Both companies ended 2009 with turnover of around $50m with Chemicon outselling ASEF for the first time since 2006.

Report writing

10 Ex ❶: T asks Ss to read the task and the sample answer. Ss then discuss whether the answer fulfils the task.

Suggested answer:
The candidate fulfils the task but not very clearly. Although he/she adheres to the word limit and recommends how to spend the profits and outlines the benefits, as required, there is no clear organisation of ideas in paragraphs. This makes the writer's ideas difficult to follow. In addition, typical elements of report writing are lacking, such as headings, bullets and standard report writing phrases.

11 Ex ❷: Ss discuss the main points they think the candidate is trying to make and the reasons he/she gives to support these ideas. In feedback, T should point out that many supporting ideas are given but they are not always organised around explicitly stated main points; the ideas are therefore difficult to follow.

Main points	*Supporting ideas*
Computers are not necessary.	*Employees already have new computers.* *The existing computers are fast enough for employees' routine work.*
Language training is a good idea.	*It would help the company increase export sales to Spain and France.* *Staff would enjoy the lessons and feel the company is investing in them.* *It would be good for motivation.*
Special bonus payments are not recommended.	*They would be good for motivation but do not invest in the company.* *Staff would expect more bonuses in the future.* *There is the question of who you give the bonuses to.*

12 Ex ❸: Ss discuss whether they think the sample answer is organised in logical paragraphs. T elicits how many paragraphs Ss think it should have and the purpose of each one.

Suggested answer:
*The report could have three main paragraphs: **Introduction**, **Areas under consideration** and **Recommendations**. The **Introduction** could briefly outline the aim of the report (to examine how the company should reinvest its profits). Within the **Areas under consideration** section, there could be three bullets, one for each proposal. Alternatively, this section could be further divided into three paragraphs, making five paragraphs in total. The **Recommendations** section could confirm which area should be invested in (language training) and outline ways the company might implement this proposal (organising French and Spanish courses etc.).*

13 Ex ❹: Ss rewrite the sample answer, focusing on clear organisation. (See the end of this unit for further information on the organisation of reports.) Before Ss write, T uses this opportunity to review report writing conventions. T may wish to refer Ss to Unit 1a and page 77 of the Student's Book of this Exam focus section for essential report writing phrases.

Sample answer: *(243 words)*

Introduction

This report sets out to examine how the company should re-invest this year's profits. The areas under consideration are the purchase of new computers, the provision of language training courses and the payment of special bonuses.

Areas under consideration

- **New computers**
  The majority of company computers are quite new and fast enough to handle the work done on them. Consequently, new computers would not be recommended.

- **Language training courses**
  The company aims to increase exports, particularly in Spain and France. Therefore, language training courses would be an excellent idea for those employees who deal with business partners and customers overseas. In addition, training courses would increase motivation: staff would enjoy the lessons and perceive that the company is investing in them. Therefore, language training would be an option.

- **Special bonus payments**
  Although special bonus payments would have a beneficial impact on motivation, they would have no direct effect on the company's operations. There are also potential problems concerning the selection of staff eligible for the payments and the setting of a precedent for future payments. Therefore, bonus payments would not be advisable.

Recommendations

It is felt that the best solution for both the company and staff would be to invest in language training. It is suggested that the company should organise courses in French and Spanish. Those employees who have contact with partners and customers should be assured of places but other interested members of staff should also be allowed to attend.

---

14 Ex ❺: T refers Ss to the **Writing Test Assessment Sheet** on page 78 of the Student's Book. Ss consider the questions in relation to their revised report. Alternatively, T may wish to ask Ss to exchange their answers and give each other feedback using the Assessment Sheet. Before the lesson, T should have made photocopies of the Assessment Sheet for Ss to use.

Formal letter writing

Exam focus: Writing Test Part Two (Letter)

For Writing Test Part Two, candidates write a 200–250 word formal business letter or report. All the points in the rubric must be included in the answer. The task tests the ability to produce an appropriate piece of extended directed writing.

For the letter, candidates are expected to plan, organise and present their ideas clearly. Letters should be divided into clear paragraphs. Although candidates should not write addresses, they are expected to know letter layout and conventions, including appropriate salutations and closures. Typical written functional phrases should be used.

15 Ex ❶: T asks Ss to read the task and the candidate's preparatory notes. Before Ss write the letter, T refers to the section on planning formal letters. T should elicit the purpose and audience of the letter, how many paragraphs might be appropriate and what information might be included in each one. T may wish to refer Ss to Unit 3a and page 77 of the Student's Book of this Exam focus section for essential letter writing phrases. (See the end of this unit for further information on planning formal letters.)

> *Sample answer:*   *(250 words)*
>
> *Dear Ricardo*
>
> *Further to our conversation of 30 March, I am writing to outline the proposed programme for your visit to our offices (12–15 April).*
>
> *On Thursday morning I will be at the airport to meet your flight and, assuming there are no delays, I will take you straight to your hotel so that you can check in and freshen up. As Mr Wilkins wishes to see you before the meeting, a business lunch has been arranged. We will then travel to the company in time for the meeting, scheduled to run from 14.30 to 18.00. After such a long day I suggest dinner at your hotel.*
>
> *Friday's meeting is due to start at 09.30. A taxi has been arranged to pick you up at the hotel at 08.50. Since the meeting lasts all day, the company will provide a working lunch. After work you will have a chance to return to your hotel before dinner at The Riverside Lodge at 20.00.*
>
> *Your name has been entered for the Golf Tournament (08.30 on Saturday morning). Mr Wilkins will collect you from your hotel at 08.00. After the competition there is a formal dinner with a distinguished speaker at 19.30.*
>
> *A taxi will collect you from your hotel at 07.30 on Sunday morning to take you to the airport in time for your 09.45 return flight.*
>
> *I look forward to meeting you on the 12th. In the meantime, please do not hesitate to contact me on 020 755 9800.*
>
> *Yours sincerely*

16 Ex ❷: T refers Ss to the **Writing Test Assessment Sheet** on page 78 of the Student's Book. Before the lesson, T may wish to make photocopies of the Assessment Sheet for Ss to use. Ss consider the questions in relation to their revised letter. Alternatively, T may wish to ask Ss to exchange their answers and give each other feedback using the Assessment Sheet.

17 T draws Ss' attention to the essential report and letter writing phrases on page 77 of the Student's Book.

Conciseness

Good professional writing is concise. It is useful to consider the following areas.

Sentence length

Clarity and conciseness are affected by sentence length. Long sentences can be confusing, especially if they contain several ideas. Ss should check the clarity of any long sentences they write; any sentence of more than twenty words is likely to be difficult to read. In business writing, people are advised to remember KISS: Keep it short and simple. In the exam, however, the candidate's mark is affected by the range of language demonstrated. Ss are therefore advised to use a variety of sentence constructions but to ensure that they check the clarity of long sentences.

Wordiness and redundancy

Ss should be encouraged to cut any unnecessary words/information, e.g. *in the following year, which was 1996*, ... Ss should also be encouraged to use shorter alternatives if they exist, e.g. *sales dropped just a little bit* can be rewritten as *sales dropped slightly*.

Reference words

Reference words, e.g. *it, they, which,* help the writer to avoid repeating words, sentences or even a whole paragraph, aiding conciseness. Ss also need to ensure their use of reference words is clear in their writing.

Ellipsis

Ellipsis refers to the omission of words when the meaning is sufficiently clear, e.g. *the next year sales went up even more quickly than they did the year before*. Repetition can be avoided through the use of ellipsis and shorter, simpler sentences can be produced.

Repetition

Any information which is repeated for no reason should be cut. Repetition of words and phrases can be avoided through the use of reference words and ellipsis.

Organisation of reports

Reports need to be organised so that the reader can get a general idea of the content quickly and can identify which section to look at in more detail for specific information.

Paragraphing

As with any writing, the writer needs to organise ideas into paragraphs. In a report, these paragraphs may take the form of separate sections or bullet points.

Layout

All reports in the exam need an overall heading. It is also helpful for the reader if the report is divided into sections with headings. Most reports need at least an *Introduction*, *Findings* or main points and a *Conclusion*. Within each section, there should be clear paragraphs and/or bullet points.

Main points and supporting ideas

The reader needs to be able to skim the report to get a quick idea of the main points. The writer needs to ensure that the reader can identify the main points and information which is simply supporting the main points. Weak candidates in the exam tend to repeat ideas rather than making clear main points and supporting them.

Linking words and phrases

The relationship between ideas needs to be made clear through the use of linking words and phrases (e.g. *however, this means that*). Ss should also use phrases to guide the reader through the whole text (e.g. *There are a number of factors which ...*).

Planning formal letters

When planning formal letters and other types of writing, the following areas should be considered.

Purpose

Before starting, a writer should always ask: *Why am I writing?* (purpose). *Is it to persuade, inform or complain? What outcome do I expect from the letter?* In the letter in the unit, the writer expects to provide clear information for the business associate. A secondary purpose is to make social contact with the visitor so that the visitor will feel relaxed upon arrival.

Audience

Another question which a writer should always ask is: *Who am I writing to?* (audience). *Is the reader an expert on the topic or will the information be difficult for him/her? Is the reader a native or non-native user of the language? What impact will these factors have on the way I write the letter?* In the letter in the unit, the reader is a non-native speaker of English and the letter therefore needs to be very clear. Layout as well as language may aid clarity. (In the exam, however, candidates need to guard against being over-simple; they need to demonstrate the range of their written language while remaining clear.)

Paragraphing

As with any writing, the writer needs to organise ideas into paragraphs. These aid clarity and make the letter more accessible.

Functional phrases

It is common to use standard functional phrases in formal letters, e.g.
Referring: *Further to your letter of ... in which ...*
Requesting: *I would be grateful if you could ...*
Inviting further contact: *Should you have any questions, please do not hesitate to contact me.*

The Speaking Test: Overview

Assessment criteria

The assessment criteria used by *Cambridge ESOL* for the Speaking Test are **Grammar and vocabulary, Discourse management, Pronunciation, Interactive communication** and **Global achievement.** These categories have been used in this unit with the exception of **Discourse management**, which refers to a candidate's ability to use English beyond sentence level. It was decided to simplify this category to make the criteria more tangible for Ss. Ss will obtain good marks for **Discourse management** if they follow the advice given under **Interactive communication** and **Linking of ideas**.

1 **Warmer (books closed):** T asks Ss what they know about the Speaking Test (length, parts, numbers of candidates/examiners etc.).

2 Ss then open their books and read through the overview. T points out that Ss are always examined in pairs, except when a centre has an unequal number of candidates. In this case, the remaining three candidates are examined together.

How to succeed

3 T asks Ss what they think the examiner is looking for in the Speaking Test. Ss' responses may include: clear pronunciation, grammatical accuracy etc. T then writes the headings **Interactive communication, Organisation of ideas, Grammar and vocabulary** and **Pronunciation** on the board and explains that these categories summarise the assessment criteria used by *Cambridge ESOL*. Ss brainstorm what is meant by these headings. T also asks Ss briefly to suggest tips for succeeding in the Speaking Test. Ss then read through the **How to succeed** section and compare their answers. T may wish to add some of the following information.

Interactive communication
Candidates are assessed on their ability to work well together in their pair/group of three. Marks are given for initiating and responding appropriately, contributing fully to the conversation and showing an ability to complete the task successfully. In Part Three of the Speaking Test, where candidates have to complete a collaborative task, the examiner will pay attention to how well Ss work together, noting their ability to sustain interaction and show sensitivity to turn-taking without the involvement of the examiner.

Organisation of ideas
Candidates are assessed on their ability to use English at and beyond sentence level. This refers to the ability to produce extended utterances and to organise ideas and speech coherently (e.g. by introducing main points and supporting ideas logically, using organising/linking words and phrases). In Part One of the test, candidates should answer the examiner's questions as fully as possible. In Part Two, candidates have the opportunity for a more extended turn when giving a one-minute talk. In Part Three, candidates are required to express and justify opinions when discussing a given topic.

Grammar and vocabulary
Marks are given for accuracy, appropriateness and range of the candidate's grammar and vocabulary.

Pronunciation
Candidates are assessed on their ability to produce comprehensible utterances. Marks are given for production of individual sounds, word and sentence stress, and intonation.

4 T then introduces Ss to the **Speaking Test Assessment Sheet** on page 83 of the Student's Book and points out any similarities with the suggestions brainstormed by Ss earlier. T emphasises that this checklist is particularly useful for Part Two (Short Talk) and Part Three (Collaborative Task) of the Speaking Test and that it will be used to provide feedback on Ss' performance throughout the course.

Personal information

5 T introduces the layout of the Speaking Test by referring Ss to the visual showing two candidates and two examiners. T should point out that Examiner 1 interviews the candidates while Examiner 2 sits slightly apart and listens to the conversation.

6 **Ex ❶**: Before the lesson, T should have photocopied cards from the back of the T's Book. Ss work in pairs. Ss take turns to pick a card and ask their partner about the topic on the card (e.g. *What do you particularly like about the company you work for?*). T should refer Ss to the **Exam tips** for Part One.

Exam focus: Speaking Test Part One

The examiner asks candidates general questions, e.g. about their home, free time or travel. Candidates are not expected to interact with each other during this part of the test.

Short talk

7 T reminds Ss of the format and aim of Part Two of the Speaking Test and refers Ss to the **Exam tips**. T may also wish to refer Ss to the **Don't forget!** section in Unit 5b, which deals with short talks.

Exam focus: Speaking Test Part Two

Each candidate chooses a topic from a list of three options (one general, one general business and one specialised business topic) and speaks about it for one minute. To avoid overlap, the candidates receive different lists. When each candidate has finished speaking, the other candidate has an opportunity to ask one or two questions. Candidates can take notes during their partner's presentations.

Candidates have one minute to think about what they want to say and should use the time to make notes. Ss are expected to plan, organise and present their ideas clearly. They should use appropriate phrases to structure their talk.

---

8 T explains that the audio CD includes both a bad and good version of Parts Two and Three of a simulated BEC Higher Speaking Test. (No audioscript is provided as the Speaking Test is so long.) The focus here is on poor and good task fulfilment. The simulation has been recorded as a whole. T therefore needs to stop the audio CD at appropriate places. Interview One on the audio CD refers to the bad version of both Part Two and Three; Interview Two refers to the good version. The audio CD also contains model answers for Part Two of the Speaking Test, these follow the simulation.

9 **Ex ❶**: Ss look at the three topics and briefly discuss which they would choose if they were doing the exam.

> (!) T should ensure that Ss are aware that there are typically two types of topic in Part Two: *How to ...* and *The importance of ...* . Ss should avoid giving a short talk which is a mixture of both. *The importance of a good hotel when travelling on business* requires the candidate to give reasons **why** a good hotel is (un)important. *How to provide good customer service* requires Ss to discuss **the methods** by which good customer service can be provided.

10 Ex ❷: Ss listen to Natacha and Salvatore making a poor attempt at Part Two of the Speaking Test and assess their performance using the Short Talk part of the **Speaking Test Assessment Sheet** on page 83 of the Student's Book. Before the lesson, T may wish to make photocopies of the Assessment Sheet.

Suggested answer:

		Natacha	Salvatore
SHORT TALK	Does the student show a clear understanding of the task?	No	No
	Is there an appropriate introduction and conclusion?	Partly	No
	Are the student's ideas well-organised and logically ordered?	No	No
	Is appropriate signposting and linking language used?	No	No
	Does the student develop ideas rather than repeat them?	No	No
	Are the ideas clearly expressed and easy to understand?	Yes	Yes
	Does the student speak in a clear and natural manner?	No	Yes
	Is the talk of an appropriate length?	Yes	No

Natacha starts well, with an introductory sentence, stating her view and giving a reason. However, she then starts simply to list facilities needed in a good hotel without explaining why they would be important. She becomes more hesitant and fizzles out at the end without a concluding comment.

*Salvatore's answer is a mixture of **The importance of ...** and **How to ...** . He only really addresses the latter when he talks about having contact before, during and after the sale. He does not have a clear introduction and conclusion and his talk is over long (1 min. 25 secs.).*

11 Ex ❸: Ss listen to the improved version and say how Natacha's and Salvatore's performance is better.

Suggested answer:
Natacha: She starts with a clear introduction. She has three clear points in the body of her talk. For each point she states an aspect of a hotel and explains why it is important. She uses clear language to signal her points and finishes with a neat conclusion.
Salvatore: His talk is now slightly short. In his opening sentence he explains the structure of his talk: he divides it into before, during and after the sale. This means that the listener can follow, even though Salvatore becomes slightly confused in the middle and refers to a 24-hour phone line as something that is available during the sale. Because of the clear chronological order, it is clear when Salvatore reaches the end even though his talk lacks a conclusion.

12 Ex ❹: T reminds Ss that during Part Two of the Speaking Test they are expected to listen to the other candidate's talk and then ask a relevant question. T points out that candidates may take notes while listening. T asks Ss to comment on the questions Natacha and Salvatore ask each other and to think of other questions.

13 Ex ❺: T points out that Natacha's talk was easy to follow because she had three main points with supporting ideas and her talk was framed with a one-sentence introduction and conclusion. T draws Ss' attention to a framework they can use to plan short talks. Ss then choose one of the three topics and spend one minute preparing a one-minute talk using the framework.

14 Ex ❻: Ss work in pairs and take turns to give their talks. As they listen to their partner, Ss complete the Short Talk section of the **Speaking Test Assessment Sheet** and give each other feedback.

Collaborative task

15 T reminds Ss of the format and aim of Part Three of the Speaking Test and refers Ss to the **Exam tips**. T also refers Ss to the visual, showing the exam layout for this part of the test. (Ss look at each other, not the examiner.)

16 **Ex ❶:** T refers Ss to the **Speaking Test Assessment Sheet** on page 83 of the Student's Book. Before the lesson, T may wish to make photocopies of the Assessment Sheet for Ss to use. Ss listen to Natacha and Salvatore making a poor attempt at Part Three of the Speaking Test and assess their performance using the Collaborative Task section of the **Speaking Test Assessment Sheet**.

Suggested answer:

		Natacha	Salvatore
COLLABORATIVE TASK	Does the student show a clear understanding of the task?	No	No
	Is there an an attempt to establish a shared context?	No	No
	Does the student give reasons to support opinions?	Partly	Partly
	Does the student listen and respond to other opinions?	Partly	Partly
	Are the student's ideas easy to understand?	Yes	Yes
	Does the student ask for clarification when necessary?	Yes	Yes
	Does the student agree and disagree appropriately and naturally?	Partly	Partly
	Does the student summarise and move the task towards a conclusion?	No	No

There are two fundamental problems. Firstly, the candidates only attempt to deal with the second part of the task; they ignore the bullet point about company representatives. Secondly, because they do not attempt to establish a shared context, they talk at cross-purposes. They need to establish who the visitors are and their objectives in entertaining them; then they can assess the suitability of any proposals made and move the discussion towards a conclusion.

17 **Ex ❷:** Ss listen to the improved version and say how Natacha and Salvatore's performance is better.

Suggested answer:
Both candidates are much better overall. They quickly establish the identity and profile of the visitors before addressing the first part of the task. They appear to understand the task and move it on towards a conclusion. They reach an agreement and summarise the main points.

18 Ex ❸: Ss read the prompts and have 30 seconds to think before they begin the task. T may wish to put Ss into groups of three: One S fills in the Collaborative Task section of the **Speaking Test Assessment Sheet** on page 83 of the Student's Book while the other Ss complete the task.

> **Exam focus: Speaking Test Part Three**
>
> This is a collaborative task. Candidates are required to have a brief guided discussion in pairs or threes. They are given a task sheet which outlines a business situation and the points which need to be discussed and decided together. Candidates have 30 seconds to prepare individually for the discussion.
>
> Candidates should start by establishing a context (e.g. the type of company they work for). They are expected to be able to initiate, respond and turn-take appropriately without intervention by the examiner. Candidates need to be aware that they are expected to move the discussion towards a decision rather than simply discuss various options.

Short talk model answers

The **audio CD** contains native speaker versions of the one-minute talks which appear in Units 5b, 7b and 8a. T may choose to play them to Ss as part of the unit in which they appear or use them as 'models' as the exam approaches. Ss should use photocopies of the Short Talk section of the **Speaking Test Assessment Sheet** to assess each talk as they listen. T may also wish to ask Ss to note down each speaker's main points and supporting ideas.

The best model is probably the speaker in Unit 8a: *The importance of a global presence.* The speaker uses a very clear introduction and conclusion and provides clear support for the points he makes. T should point out that because of time constraints, introductions and conclusions should be one (or maximum two) sentences long. T should also point out how the speakers clearly fulfil the task: the *How to ...* talks give clear methods, *The importance of ...* talks give clear reasons.

Model answers

Unit 5b   One-minute talk: How to fill a key vacancy

	Does the student show a clear understanding of the task?	Yes
	Is there an appropriate introduction and conclusion?	Partly
	Are the student's ideas well-organised and logically ordered?	Yes
SHORT TALK	Is appropriate signposting and linking language used?	Yes
	Does the student develop ideas rather than repeat them?	Yes
	Are the ideas clearly expressed and easy to understand?	Yes
	Does the student speak in a clear and natural manner?	Yes
	Is the talk of an appropriate length?	Yes

> *The speaker begins with an introductory sentence about the standard procedure used for recruitment. The speaker then goes through the procedure chronologically, using clear sequencing language. The ending would be clearer if the speaker used a concluding sentence.*

Unit 5b   One-minute talk: The importance of having a good CV

SHORT TALK	Does the student show a clear understanding of the task?	Yes
	Is there an appropriate introduction and conclusion?	Yes
	Are the student's ideas well-organised and logically ordered?	Yes
	Is appropriate signposting and linking language used?	Yes
	Does the student develop ideas rather than repeat them?	Yes
	Are the ideas clearly expressed and easy to understand?	Yes
	Does the student speak in a clear and natural manner?	Yes
	Is the talk of an appropriate length?	No

Even though the talk is slightly too short (50 seconds), the speaker conveys her message effectively. She starts with an introductory sentence about the importance of a good CV then makes four points demonstrating why it is important. She finishes with a clear concluding sentence.

Unit 7b   One-minute talk: How to encourage ethical behaviour from employees

SHORT TALK	Does the student show a clear understanding of the task?	Yes
	Is there an appropriate introduction and conclusion?	Partly
	Are the student's ideas well-organised and logically ordered?	Yes
	Is appropriate signposting and linking language used?	Yes
	Does the student develop ideas rather than repeat them?	Yes
	Are the ideas clearly expressed and easy to understand?	Yes
	Does the student speak in a clear and natural manner?	Yes
	Is the talk of an appropriate length?	Yes

*The speaker begins with an introduction about the importance of ethical behaviour and then says the key question is how to ensure it. He then makes five points, some of them ordered chronologically. The end of his talk is clear as he begins his last point with **Finally ...** . However, the talk would be neater with a more obvious conclusion.*

Unit 7b   One-minute talk: The importance of ethics in today's business world

1.39

SHORT TALK		
	Does the student show a clear understanding of the task?	Yes
	Is there an appropriate introduction and conclusion?	No
	Are the student's ideas well-organised and logically ordered?	Partly
	Is appropriate signposting and linking language used?	Partly
	Does the student develop ideas rather than repeat them?	Yes
	Are the ideas clearly expressed and easy to understand?	Yes
	Does the student speak in a clear and natural manner?	Yes
	Is the talk of an appropriate length?	Yes

The speaker makes three clear points about the importance of ethics. However, the beginning is rather confusing as there is no introduction and it is difficult at first to see the relevance of what he says. The talk also finishes abruptly and would benefit from an obvious conclusion.

Unit 8a   One-minute talk: The importance of a global presence

1.40

SHORT TALK		
	Does the student show a clear understanding of the task?	Yes
	Is there an appropriate introduction and conclusion?	Yes
	Are the student's ideas well-organised and logically ordered?	Yes
	Is appropriate signposting and linking language used?	Yes
	Does the student develop ideas rather than repeat them?	Yes
	Are the ideas clearly expressed and easy to understand?	Yes
	Does the student speak in a clear and natural manner?	Yes
	Is the talk of an appropriate length?	Yes

The speaker makes clear points, with a clear introduction and conclusion.

Unit 8a   One-minute talk: How to promote an imported brand

1.41

SHORT TALK		
	Does the student show a clear understanding of the task?	Yes
	Is there an appropriate introduction and conclusion?	Yes
	Are the student's ideas well-organised and logically ordered?	Yes
	Is appropriate signposting and linking language used?	Yes
	Does the student develop ideas rather than repeat them?	Yes
	Are the ideas clearly expressed and easy to understand?	Yes
	Does the student speak in a clear and natural manner?	Yes
	Is the talk of an appropriate length?	Yes

The speaker makes clear points, with a clear introduction and conclusion.

Unit 8a   One-minute talk: The importance of stereotypes in advertising

SHORT TALK	Does the student show a clear understanding of the task?	*Yes*
	Is there an appropriate introduction and conclusion?	*Partly*
	Are the student's ideas well-organised and logically ordered?	*Yes*
	Is appropriate signposting and linking language used?	*Yes*
	Does the student develop ideas rather than repeat them?	*Yes*
	Are the ideas clearly expressed and easy to understand?	*Yes*
	Does the student speak in a clear and natural manner?	*Yes*
	Is the talk of an appropriate length?	*Yes*

The speaker begins with a clear introduction and makes clear points. The examples given support the points he makes. The end of his talk is clear as he begins his final point with **Lastly ...** *. However, the talk might benefit from a more obvious conclusion.*

Unit 5a Staff motivation

Objectives:	To enable Ss to talk about motivation at work
	To practise reading for gist and specific information
	To practise listening for gist
	To practise report writing
	To review formal language

Unit overview

- ### What motivates staff?

Speaking	Ss discuss general statements about motivation at work.
Reading	Ss read an article on motivational techniques to identify and discuss the writer's attitude.
Speaking	Ss discuss answers to questions on the article.

- ### A motivation survey

Listening	Ss listen to five employees talk about motivation as part of a company survey and decide what grievance each speaker has (*Listening Test Part Two*).
Language	Ss focus on formal language.
Writing	Ss read the audioscript and decide which grievances to include in the report findings. Ss then complete the *Findings* section in an appropriate style (*Writing Test Part Two*).
	Ss complete the *Recommendations* section of the report (*Writing Test Part Two*).
Optional task	Ss design a questionnaire on motivation in their English lessons.

What motivates staff?

1   Ex ❶: Ss read the two statements and explain why they agree/do not agree with them. Ss then look at the suggestions for ways of motivating staff and rank them in order of importance. Encourage them to give reasons for their choice of ranking order.

2   Ex ❷: Ss read the article on staff motivation. T elicits the writer's attitude to motivational techniques and asks Ss if they share his attitude.

> *Suggested answer:*
> *The writer is sceptical. He sees so-called 'new' motivational techniques as old ideas repackaged. He also questions whether these techniques are ever put into practice successfully.*

3   Ex ❸: Ss read the article again and discuss the questions in the handwritten notes. The questions are not comprehension questions but prompts for discussion.

Supplementary activity

T asks Ss to order the motivational techniques according to which they believe to be most effective. Ss can number the seven boxes from 1 to 7.

A motivation survey

4   Ex ❶: This exercise practises the skills needed for Listening Test Part Two. T asks Ss to read through the list of grievances and think of words or phrases they would expect to hear connected with each one. For example, for *uninteresting work*, Ss might expect to hear words and phrases such as *it's boring, monotonous, dull*. Ss then listen and match each speaker with a grievance.

1 H	2 F	3 E	4 B	5 C

Exam focus: Listening Test Part Two

Candidates listen to five short topic-related extracts and complete two tasks, which may involve identifying any combination of the following for each extract: speaker, topic, function, opinion or feelings. The five extracts are heard twice. Both tasks test candidates' ability to listen for gist and specific information.

Candidates should be aware that each extract contains both a Task One answer and a Task Two answer. Some candidates may prefer to deal with Task One during the first listening and Task Two during the second listening, or they may choose to attempt the two tasks simultaneously. For each task, they have a list of eight options to choose from. Incorrect options are included in the recordings in order to distract unwary candidates.

This exercise differs from the exam in that here there is only one task. In the exam itself candidates have to do two tasks simultaneously as they listen to each extract.

---

5   Ex ❷: In this exercise Ss will focus on features of formal language, which will help them in their writing. T asks Ss to search through the incomplete report to find examples of the points related to formal language. T should point out that the reports which Ss have to write in the exam do not need to be extremely formal; however, the style needs to be consistent. (See the end of this unit for further information on formal language.)

Passives
The findings are based on interviews ...
Unless these issues are addressed ...

Impersonal language
The above examples of the passive plus the following:
This report presents the results of ...
It is clear that ...
... there are significant levels of dissatisfaction

Formal vocabulary
findings, significant levels, regarding, certain issues, addressed, as a matter of urgency, consequent, undoubtedly

Noun phrases
survey of staff motivation
levels of dissatisfaction
consequent demotivation
negative impact on the performance of the company

6   **Ex ❸:** Ss discuss the main grievances of the Terrain employees. T may wish to refer Ss back to the audioscript at this stage. Ss then complete the *Findings* section of the report by summarising the grievances. When setting this task, T may wish to refer Ss back to Unit 1 and Exam focus: Writing (page 77 of the Student's Book) for useful report phrases. (See the end of this unit for a sample answer.)

(!)   T should draw Ss' attention to the need for consistency in bullet points, e.g. if the first bullet starts with an infinitive, so should all the other bullets.

Exam focus: Writing Test Part Two (Report)

For Writing Test Part Two, candidates write a 200–250 word proposal, piece of business correspondence or report. All the points in the rubric must be included in the answer. To generate the range of language required at this level, the task input is broad and non-specific, which means that a reasonably high background knowledge is needed by the candidate. To ensure that no candidate is disadvantaged a choice of tasks is given. The task tests the ability to produce an appropriate piece of extended directed writing.

For the report, candidates are expected to plan, organise and present their ideas clearly. Reports should be clearly set out, with paragraphs, headings (e.g. *Introduction, Findings, Conclusion*) and bullet points where appropriate. All reports are expected to have a title.

---

7   **Ex ❹:** Ss discuss the recommendations they would make to address the grievances. Ss then complete the *Recommendations* section of the report. If time is short, T may wish to set this exercise as homework. If Ss do the written task in class, T may wish to ask Ss to exchange their answers in pairs and give each other feedback. (See the end of this unit for a sample answer.)

8   T asks Ss to check the completed report for word length; the pre-written sections of the report used seventy-three words and the overall word limit for the report in the exam is 200–250 words. Ss should also check that their sections of the report are written to the same level of formality as the pre-written sections.

9   **Ex ❺:** Once again, the Optional Task is designed to link the lesson with the outside world. Ss design a questionnaire to find what motivates their fellow students. T may wish to set a limit for the number of questions Ss are expected to produce. T may also wish to ask Ss to conduct their surveys and write a 200–250 word report on their findings.

Formal language

The following features of formal language are often found in reports and formal letters.

Passives

Passives are used when the writer wishes to be impersonal and also sometimes to add formality to a text. Ss should not use the passive automatically in formal letters or reports but should consider whether it is appropriate in each situation.

Impersonal language

In addition to passives, formal reports often use impersonal phrases such as *It is important that ... , It would be advisable to ... , There is no basis for ...* . Such impersonal language can be very useful, particularly when making strong recommendations or criticisms; the writer can make a point forcefully without being personal, e.g. *It is essential that action is taken immediately.*

Formal vocabulary

Ss need to develop an awareness of formal/informal vocabulary. They need to know that certain common items used in speech, e.g. *really, OK, nice* are not typical of formal writing; nor are phrasal verbs, e.g. *look up*. They need to be aware that words based on Latin are usually more formal than non-Latinate words, e.g. *terminate/end*. Imprecise words tend to be less formal than more precise equivalents, e.g. *way/method*.

Noun phrases

It is often neater and more concise to use a phrase involving a noun/group of nouns rather than a longer phrase containing a verb/several verbs, e.g. *The staff feel deeply unhappy that management do not recognise their efforts* can be phrased more neatly as *A key staff complaint is lack of recognition.*

A motivation survey Ex ❸:

Sample answer: *(116 words)*

Findings

A number of employees clearly suffer from a lack of motivation as a result of dissatisfaction in one or more areas of their work. The key findings are outlined below:

- *Staff feel undervalued by the company, both on a financial and a personal level. It is generally felt that the company's competitors offer higher levels of remuneration. The perception that managers are unappreciative of staff efforts is particularly noticeable in the Sales Department.*
- *Certain employees feel under-challenged. The company is clearly not exploiting the potential of its human resources.*
- *There appears to be a breakdown of communication in the Production Department. The confusion and resultant ill-feeling towards managers has the potential to disrupt production cycles.*

A motivation survey Ex ❹:

Sample answer: *(53 words)*

Recommendations

We strongly recommend the following measures:

- *an evaluation of job profiles throughout the company to assess whether skills could be utilised more efficiently*
- *a review of the current salary structure involving comparison with similar organisations.*

It is also essential to investigate and take action regarding communication in the Production and Sales Departments.

Unit 5b Recruitment

Objectives:	To enable Ss to talk about recruitment
	To practise text level reading skills
	To practise a collaborative speaking task
	To practise listening for specific information
	To practise giving a short talk
	To practise letter writing

Unit overview

- **Recruitment methods**

Speaking	Ss briefly discuss various recruitment methods.
Reading	Ss match functions with sentences in a text.
	Ss complete gaps in the rest of the text with appropriate sentences (*Reading Test Part Two*).
	Ss focus on reference words.
Speaking	Ss discuss the best way of recruiting a replacement for a key role in their company (*Speaking Test Part Three*).

- **The headhunting process**

Listening	Ss listen to a talk about headhunting and complete notes (*Listening Test Part One*).
	Ss listen again and make notes on how they think the talk was planned.
Speaking	Ss prepare and give a one-minute talk (*Speaking Test Part Two*).
Writing	Ss write a letter of application (*Writing Test Part Three*).

Recruitment methods

1 Warmer (optional): T asks Ss how they were recruited or found their current position.

2 Ex ❶: T elicits the advantages and disadvantages of the methods listed. To save time, T may wish to assign one method per pair.

Suggested answer:

	Advantages	Disadvantages
Internal recruitment	The candidates already know the job and the company.	No new impetus. The same mindset. An internal candidate is not necessarily the best person on the market.
Job advertisements	Wide audience. Can potentially reach the best on the market. Fresh attitudes.	High processing costs: a large number of applicants need to be processed.
Recruitment agencies	Can be selective Can potentially get the best person for the job quickly.	Expensive.
Headhunting	Can select high quality candidates. Headhunters know the market and the best people. Can access people not actively on the job market.	Very expensive in the short term.

3 Ex ❷: T introduces Ss to Reading Test Part Two. Ss look at the functions before reading the article. T may wish to clarify the difference between 'comparing', where similarities are highlighted, and 'contrasting', where differences are highlighted. Ss then read the paragraphs and match the sentences with the functions.

a emphasising   b exemplifying   c comparing   d explaining   e contrasting

---

Exam focus: Reading Test Part Two

Candidates read a 450–500 word text and complete the six gaps from a choice of eight sentences. Sentence H is the example sentence and one other sentence is a distractor and does not fit any of the gaps. This tests the ability to read for detail and understand text structure.

Candidates read the whole text for general understanding and then the options. They re-read the text and fill any gaps they feel sure of, always reading before and after a gap to ensure a sentence fits appropriately. They then concentrate on any remaining gaps. Finally, they read their completed text, checking overall coherence, grammatical agreement and cohesive devices such as linking words (e.g. *however*) and reference words (e.g. *this*).

Both Ex ❷ and Ex ❸ develop skills which are relevant for Reading Test Part Two. However, only Ex ❸ is similar to the task in the exam.

---

4 Ex ❸: Ss read the second part of the article and choose the best sentence to fill each gap.

1 B   2 E   3 A   4 F

5 **Ex ❹:** T elicits examples of reference words (e.g. *it, them, such*). Ss then read the text again and underline any reference words. T elicits which of the reference words refer to passages of text rather than single words.

> *Most of the reference words refer clearly to the preceding single nouns. The only ones which refer to a passage of text are the following.*
>
> **This:** *referring to the belief that traditional advertising would not be specific enough (Para. 1, line 5)*
> **This information:** *referring to the information gained by the headhunter navigating round the department (Para. 3, line 5)*
> **all of this:** *referring to everything mentioned in the preceding paragraphs (Para. 4, line 1)* **this process:** *referring to the process of keeping a record of all names (Para. 4, line 2)*

> (!) T may wish to point out that Taps.com has been taken over by Stepstone.com, the internet recruitment company.

6 **Ex ❺:** This exercise practises the skills needed for Speaking Test Part Three. Ss establish a context and try to reach agreement on the qualities required for the job and the best method of recruiting a replacement. T may wish to assess Ss' performance using the Collaborative Task section of the **Speaking Test Assessment Sheet** on page 83 of the Student's Book.

> (!) T should ensure that the Assessment Sheet has been clearly presented to Ss. (See T's notes for the **How to succeed** section of **Exam focus: Speaking** for further information.)

Exam focus: Speaking Test Part Three

This is a collaborative task. Candidates are required to have a brief guided discussion in pairs or threes. They are given a task sheet which outlines a business situation and the points which need to be discussed and decided together. Candidates have 30 seconds to prepare individually for the discussion.

Candidates should start by establishing a context (e.g. the type of company they work for). They are expected to be able to initiate, respond and turn-take appropriately without intervention by the examiner. Candidates need to be aware that they are expected to move the discussion towards a decision rather than simply discuss various options.

The headhunting process

7 **Ex ❶**: This exercise practises the skills needed for Listening Test Part One. T asks Ss to read through the notes and predict what sort of information or word types could be used to complete each sentence. Ss listen and complete the notes.

 These answers are bolded in T's audioscript.

1 agency recruitment	2 skills shortages
3 desk research	4 neutral location
5 presents his findings	6 offer process
7 first annual salary	8 a retainer
9 strengths and weaknesses	10 key players
11 (commercially) sensitive	12 motivated

Exam focus: Listening Test Part One

Candidates listen to a monologue (or a series of long turns by more than one speaker) and complete each of the gaps in the text with up to three words or a number. There are twelve gaps in total. The recording is heard twice. This task tests the ability to listen for and note specific information.

Candidates have 45 seconds to read through the input before listening and should use the time to think about what might fit in the gaps. The questions follow the order of the recording. Candidates are expected to write the **exact words** used in the recording. Provided that the words written are recognisable, candidates are not penalised for incorrect spelling.

---

8 **Ex ❷**: T points out to Ss that Dave's talk is a standard presentation rather than a one-minute talk as in the exam. However, the points in the **Don't forget!** section are relevant for all short talks. Ss read the questions, listen to the audio CD again and answer the questions.

Exam focus: Speaking Test Part Two

Each candidate chooses a topic from a list of three options (one general, one general business and one specialised business topic) and speaks about it for one minute. To avoid overlap, the candidates receive different lists. When each candidate has finished speaking, the other candidate has an opportunity to ask one or two questions. Candidates can take notes during their partner's presentations.

Candidates have one minute to think about what they want to say and should use the time to make notes. Ss are expected to plan, organise and present their ideas clearly. They should use appropriate phrases to structure their talk.

This exercise differs from the exam in that here there are only two topics to choose from. In the exam itself candidates choose from three options.

The headhunting process Ex ❷:

Suggested answer:

Purpose
To explain how headhunting works and illustrate its benefits.

Content
Dave's main points include an overview of recruitment methods in general, the headhunting process, remuneration and the benefits of using headhunters. Sometimes he does not support his main points; they are sufficient in themselves. At other times, Dave supports his point by giving more detail (e.g. about the advantages of using a headhunter in the penultimate paragraph). At times Dave rephrases what he has said for emphasis (e.g. the final sentence).

Organisation
Dave orders his main points by giving an overview of how his area fits in with other recruitment methods. He then talks through the chronological sequence of headhunting. Finally, he stresses the benefits of headhunting. Dave introduces his talk by introducing himself and describing his topic. He concludes by stressing to the audience the benefits of what he does.

Language
Dave uses linking words and phrases in the following areas: sequencing words (first, then, afterwards, when, finally), explaining/rephrasing (which is, otherwise known as, in other words) and emphasising (this is particularly the case in ...). He also uses phrases to signpost his talk (I'm here to tell you a little bit about ...) and signal what follows (The advantage of a good headhunter is that ...).

9 **Ex ❸:** This exercise practises the skills needed for Speaking Test Part Two. When setting up this task, T may wish to refer Ss to the framework for planning short talks on page 81 of the Student's Book. Ss take turns to make and listen to each other's short talks. Those listening should be encouraged to make notes and ask questions at the end. T may wish to ask Ss to use the Short Talk section of the **Speaking Test Assessment Sheet** on page 83 of the Student's Book to evaluate each other's performance. Before the lesson, T should have made photocopies of the Assessment Sheet for Ss to use. Once Ss have completed their own talks, play the audio CD which contains example models of each talk. (See T's notes for Exam focus: Speaking for further information for suggestions on how to use the models.)

1.23–1.24

10 Ex ❹: This exercise practises the skills needed for Writing Test Part Two. T may wish to ask Ss to prepare a detailed plan in class showing how they intend to organise their ideas before they write the letter for homework. When setting up this task, T may wish to refer Ss back to Unit 3a and Exam focus: Writing (page 77 of the Student's Book) for useful letter phrases. Ss are not expected to provide a CV but T may like to ask Ss to hand in the job advert with their homework. (See the end of this unit for a sample letter.)

Exam focus: Writing Test Part Two (Letter)

For Writing Test Part Two, candidates write a 200–250 word proposal, piece of business correspondence or report. All the points in the rubric must be included in the answer. To generate the range of language required at this level, the task input is broad and non-specific, which means that a reasonably high background knowledge is needed by the candidate. To ensure that no candidate is disadvantaged a choice of tasks is given. The task tests the ability to produce an appropriate piece of extended directed writing.

For the letter, candidates are expected to plan, organise and present their ideas clearly. Letters should be divided into clear paragraphs. Although candidates should not write addresses, they are expected to know letter layout and conventions, including appropriate salutations and closures. Typical written functional phrases should be used.

The headhunting process Ex ❹:

Sample answer: (234 words)

Dear Mr Jacobs

I am writing to apply for the position of Sales Adviser for the North East Region which was advertised in the Herald International yesterday.

Although I am currently working in the Marketing Department of a large multinational, I would appreciate the opportunity to work for a rapidly expanding young company such as yours.

As you can see from my enclosed CV, I obtained an honours degree in Sales and Marketing from Nottingham University in 2004. I thoroughly enjoyed the six months I spent working in Sales at Boots plc as part of the course. During this time I gained invaluable insights into the nature of sales. After leaving university I initially spent time working for a small local firm before finding my current job and I feel that I am more suited to the dynamics and varied demands of a smaller firm.

Not only has my work experience familiarised me with the challenges faced by the industry today but, having been brought up in the north east, I know the region, its problems and its undoubted potential. As a result, I feel that I would be able to relate to your customers on both a professional and a personal level.

I am available for interview from 15 September and would be pleased to discuss my CV with you in more detail then.

I look forward to hearing from you.

Yours sincerely

Unit 6a Corporate culture

Objectives:	To enable Ss to talk about company culture
	To practise reading and listening for specific information
	To review gerunds and infinitives

Unit overview

- ### What shapes corporate culture?

Speaking	Ss discuss what certain factors reveal about a companys' culture.
Reading	Ss read an extract from an IKEA brochure and make notes about IKEA's corporate culture.
Language	Ss focus on gerunds and infinitives.
Speaking	Ss discuss similarities and differences between their company's and IKEA's culture.

- ### The IKEA way

Listening 1	Ss listen to the Managing Director of IKEA UK talk about the company's culture and answer multiple-choice comprehension questions (*Listening Test Part Three*).
Speaking	Ss discuss what their company does to promote its corporate culture.
Listening 2	Ss listen to five IKEA managers tell anecdotes about the company and match them with IKEA's core values.
Speaking	Ss identify their company's values and illustrate them with anecdotes.
Writing	Ss write a statement of their company's values.
Optional task	Ss visit the IKEA website and prepare a presentation of the company's history.

What shapes corporate culture?

1 **Ex ❶:** T asks Ss what the four items tell them about a company's culture. T acknowledges that not all of the items are applicable to all companies, e.g. not all companies have a mission statement.

> *Suggested answer:*
> **Mission statement:** *Clearly explains a company's goals and focus. The fact that a company has a formal mission statement suggests it is organised and keen on promoting a cohesive attitude within the staff. The fact that the mission statement needs to be explicit may suggest there is some diversity of attitudes within the staff.*
> **Organisational hierarchy:** *Can show how traditional a company is, whether power is centralised and the extent to which employees are empowered.*
> **Company buildings:** *Can reflect attitudes to hierarchy and relative importance of staff, e.g. through impressive offices, separate floors or separate dining room for senior staff.*
> **Dress code:** *Can influence or reflect the degree of formality in a company.*

2 **Ex ❷:** Ss read the extract from the IKEA brochure and take notes.

> *Suggested answer:*
> **Company values:** *simplicity, humility, thrift, responsibility, enthusiasm, flexibility, openness*
> **Company policies:** *absence of status symbols (e.g. no first-class hotels, directors' dining rooms or flashy cars), recruitment of people who share the company's values, internal promotion, listening to and encouraging new ideas and initiatives, managers being involved in details*
> **Staff profile:** *People share IKEA's basic values and are also strong enough to question and change things if necessary. People are both internally promoted and recruited from outside. People have a sense of responsibility and can follow things up. Managers need to be willing to be involved in detail.*

3 **Ex ❸:** T refers Ss to the example sentences. Ss then look through the brochure extract to find further examples of gerunds and infinitives and discuss how they are used. Ss should be encouraged to categorise examples of these forms rather than discuss every occurrence separately. (See the end of this unit for further information on gerunds and infinitives.)

> (!) T may wish to point out that the writer has taken licence with the language in the text (as often happens in promotional material): many sentences are extremely short. This means that the uses of the gerund or infinitive may be difficult to identify. For example, in *Being able to praise and rebuke* at the end of Para. 5, the gerund is used not because *being* is the subject of the sentence but because it follows on from *means* in the previous sentence.

4 **Ex ❹:** Ss discuss in what ways their company culture is similar or different to that of IKEA. (T is advised to keep this discussion relatively general; specific examples illustrating company culture could overlap with **Ex ❹** on the following page, in which Ss tell anecdotes illustrating company values.)

The IKEA way

5 **Ex ❶:** This exercise practises the skills needed for Listening Test Part Three. T asks Ss to read through the questions before listening. When checking the answers, T may wish to ask Ss to identify where the answers appeared in the audioscript.

1 A	2 C	3 B	4 C
5 B	6 A	7 B	8 C

> **Exam focus: Listening Test Part Three**
>
> Candidates listen to a 3–4 minute recording of two or three speakers and answer eight multiple-choice questions. The recording is heard twice. This task tests ability to listen for specific information.
>
> The questions follow the order of the recording and are clearly signposted by the speaker(s). Incorrect options are included in the recording in order to distract unwary candidates.

6 **Ex ❷:** Ss discuss what their company does to promote its corporate culture.

7 **Ex ❸:** T explains that this exercise does not resemble an exam task; however, it provides useful practice in listening for gist. Before listening, T asks Ss to read through the IKEA company values in **Ex ❷** on the first page of the unit. Ss listen and decide which core values each anecdote illustrates.

> *Suggested answer:*
> *Speaker 1: simplicity, humility, a sense of responsibility*
> *Speaker 2: simplicity, openness*
> *Speaker 3: humility, openness, enthusiasm, simplicity*
> *Speaker 4: simplicity*
> *Speaker 5: thrift*

8 **Ex ❹:** Ss think of an anecdote to illustrate their company's core values and tell the group.

9 **Ex ❺:** Ss write a statement of their company's culture. T should point out to Ss that this writing task is more specific than in the exam. However, it provides valuable practice for the Writing Test. T may wish to ask Ss to prepare a detailed plan in class showing how they intend to organise their ideas before they write the statement for homework. If Ss do the writing task in class, T may wish to ask Ss to exchange statements and give each other feedback. (See the end of this unit for a sample answer.)

10 Ex ❻: Once again, the Optional Task is designed to link the lesson with the outside world. Ss prepare a brief presentation about IKEA's history and global expansion.

The IKEA website is easy to navigate around and Ss should have no problems finding the relevant information.

Gerunds and infinitives

The uses of the gerund and infinitive which appear in the text are as follows.

Gerunds
- **When the verb is the subject of the sentence:**
  Keeping our culture alive is management's key task.
- **After prepositions:**
  *Our corporate culture is based on a natural way **of** working and being together.*
- **After certain verbs:**
  *Caring **means** listening and encouraging new ideas.*

Infinitives
- **After certain verbs:**
  *Our customers don't **expect** to pay for first-class hotels.*
- **After modals** (without to):
  *Our managers **must** know their job.*
- **After *enough*:**
  *We also want people ... who are strong **enough** to question, renew and change.*
- **To indicate purpose:**
  *There are no status symbols **to create** barriers between managers and their fellow workers.*
- **After certain nouns:**
  *A great deal depends on our managers' perceptiveness and **ability** to care.*
- **In an introductory phrase with *is*:**
  ***The best way is** to set a good example and care about the employees.*

T may like to draw Ss' attention to further patterns with gerunds and infinitives.

Gerunds
- **After certain expressions,** e.g. *It's no use, It's not worth*
- **After *to* when used as a preposition,** e.g. *I look forward to, the key to, to be used to*

Infinitives
- **After certain adjectives,** e.g. *difficult, easy, ready*
- **After *too* + word,** e.g. *too much, too weak*

Ss should be encouraged to learn which verbs are followed by gerunds and which by infinitives.
e.g. **Gerunds:** *appreciate, avoid, consider, delay, postpone, risk, suggest*
    Infinitives: *afford, choose, decide, manage, plan, refuse, tend*

Useful nouns followed by the **infinitive** are: *decision, thing, time.*

Although some verbs, such as *like*, can be followed by either gerunds or infinitives with little effect on meaning, Ss need to be aware of those verbs where the choice does affect meaning significantly.

e.g. *I **remember** sending him the fax.*   To refer back to a specific past action
    *I must **remember** to send the fax today.*   To refer to a future action

  *Promotion will **mean** working longer hours.*   When *mean = involve*
  *He didn't **mean** to delete the file.*   When *mean = intend*

  *We **tried** cutting costs – but profits didn't improve.*   We tried out a possible way of reaching our objective.

  *We **tried** to improve profits.*   We attempted to reach our objective.

The IKEA way Ex ❺:

Sample answer: *(226 words)*

Limitless Horizons, our travel agency and advisory service specialising in adventure holidays in remote locations, was founded in 2001 by Rob Davies. We do not arrange accommodation in well-known resorts, thus encouraging travellers to discover the real country they are visiting. We constantly seek out new adventure holidays which will allow travellers to mix with local people rather than retreat to the beach or their hotel.

Although all our advice is impartial, it is influenced by certain core values:

- *Respect for local values and practices*
- *Respect for individual needs and independence*
- *Belief in the need to limit the environmental impact of our activities.*

We believe that as privileged visitors to sometimes fragile environments, we should take nothing but photographs and leave nothing but footprints.

Wherever possible, we encourage the use of small independent companies. We also insist on local guides and seek to house travellers in modest accommodation. Our clients can look forward to living the local culture and eating the local cuisine; Limitless Horizons rejects the concept of the Coca-Cola trek.

Our representatives are constantly travelling in order to update and check our information. These trips are funded solely by Limitless Horizons. We pay our way, accepting no hand-outs or free flights, thus ensuring that the only factors influencing our advice to you are your needs and those of the area you wish to visit.

Unit 6b Cultural diversity

Objectives:	To enable Ss to talk about cultural differences
	To practise text level reading skills
	To practise reading for specific information
	To practise a collaborative speaking task
	To practise letter writing
	To review language for agreeing/disagreeing
Materials needed:	Cards **six cards; one set of cards per group to be photocopied**

Unit overview

- **How culture influences business**

Speaking	Ss discuss criteria for decisions in four HR areas in their country.
Reading 1	Ss complete gaps in a newspaper article with appropriate sentences (*Reading Test Part Two*).
Speaking	Ss discuss the four areas further.
Reading 2	Ss read the results of a survey to complete a table.
Speaking	Ss discuss the difficulties people from two different countries might experience when working together.

- **Building international teams**

Speaking	Ss discuss recruiting an international sales team (*Speaking Test Part Three*).
Language	Ss focus on language for agreeing/disagreeing.
Writing	Ss write a letter to a business partner giving advice on doing business in their country (*Writing Test Part Two*).
Optional task	Ss research doing business in a foreign country and prepare a brief presentation.

How culture influences business

1   **Ex ❶**: Ss discuss the factors which affect management decision-making in the four areas of human resources in their country. T may wish to ask questions to generate discussion, e.g. *Would you recruit/ promote your family or friends even if they weren't the best people for the job?*

2   **Ex ❷**: This exercise practises the skills needed for Reading Test Part Two. Ss read the text and choose the best sentence to fill each gap.

1 F	*2 A*	*3 C*	*4 G*	*5 B*	*6 D*

> **Exam focus: Reading Test Part Two**
>
> Candidates read a 450–500 word text and complete the six gaps from a choice of eight sentences. Sentence H is the example sentence and one other sentence is a distractor and does not fit any of the gaps. This tests the ability to read for detail and understand text structure.
>
> Candidates read the whole text for general understanding and then the options. They re-read the text and fill any gaps they feel sure of, always reading before and after a gap to ensure a sentence fits appropriately. They then concentrate on any remaining gaps. Finally, they read their completed text, checking overall coherence, grammatical agreement and cohesive devices such as linking words (e.g. *however*) and reference words (e.g. *this*).

3   **Ex ❸**: Ss discuss whether decisions affecting the four areas are based on group or market logic in their culture.

4   **Ex ❹**: Ss read the conclusions and match a country with a colour from the table in **Ex ❹**. T points out that this exercise is fundamentally a logic problem: Ss identify the obvious colours from the descriptions; the rest is a process of elimination.

England – blue	*France – brown*	*Germany – purple*
Italy – yellow	*Spain – red*	

5   **Ex ❺**: Ss choose two of the five countries and discuss the difficulties people from these countries might experience when working together. For example, Germany and France are at opposite extremes on the table in **Ex ❹** regarding their attitudes towards renumeration. This could cause problems with German managers wishing to reward an individual for successful performance. In contrast, their French colleagues might prefer to reward the successful performance of the whole group.

Building international teams

6 **Ex ❶:** This exercise practises the skills needed for Speaking Test Part Three. Ss establish a context and try to reach agreement on a recruitment policy for a new joint venture. T may wish to assess Ss' performance using the Collaborative Task section of the **Speaking Test Assessment Sheet** on page 83 of the Student's Book.

> (!) T should ensure that any Assessment Sheets have been presented clearly to Ss. (See T's notes for the **How to succeed** sections of **Exam focus: Speaking** and **Exam focus: Writing**.)

Alternative activity

T may wish to use this exercise for a mini-meeting. Before the lesson, T should have photocopied cards from the back of the T's Book. T gives each S a role-card describing the speaker's cultural values. Ss should behave in accordance with the information on their cards (without revealing it to the other Ss). After the meeting, Ss guess the cultural values of the other speakers.

---

7 When setting up this task, T should refer Ss to the **Don't forget!** section. Although some books teach special **phrases** for agreeing and disagreeing, it is probably more useful for T to emphasise the **skills** involved in agreeing/disagreeing effectively.

Exam focus: Speaking Test Part Three

This is a collaborative task. Candidates are required to have a brief guided discussion in pairs or threes. They are given a task sheet which outlines a business situation and the points which need to be discussed and decided together. Candidates have 30 seconds to prepare individually for the discussion.

Candidates should start by establishing a context (e.g. the type of company they work for). They are expected to be able to initiate, respond and turn-take appropriately without intervention by the examiner. Candidates need to be aware that they are expected to move the discussion towards a decision rather than simply discuss various options.

---

8 **Ex ❷:** This exercise practises the skills needed for Writing Test Part Two. T may wish to ask Ss to prepare a detailed plan in class showing how they intend to organise their ideas before they write a letter for homework. When setting up this task, T may wish to refer Ss back to Unit 3a and Exam focus: Writing (page 77 of the Student's Book) for useful letter phrases. If Ss do the writing task in class, T may wish to ask Ss to exchange letters and give each other feedback using the **Writing Test Assessment Sheet** on page 78 of the Student's Book. Before the lesson, T should have made photocopies of the Assessment Sheet for Ss to use. (See the end of this unit for a sample letter.)

Exam focus: Writing Test Part Two (Letter)

For Writing Test Part Two, candidates write a 200–250 word proposal, piece of business correspondence or report. All the points in the rubric must be included in the answer. To generate the range of language required at this level, the task input is broad and non-specific, which means that a reasonably high background knowledge is needed by the candidate. To ensure that no candidate is disadvantaged a choice of tasks is given. The task tests the ability to produce an appropriate piece of extended directed writing.

For the letter, candidates are expected to plan, organise and present their ideas clearly. Letters should be divided into clear paragraphs. Although candidates should not write addresses, they are expected to know letter layout and conventions, including appropriate salutations and closures. Typical written functional phrases should be used.

---

9 **Ex ❸:** Once again, the Optional Task is designed to link the lesson with the outside world. Ss choose a country and use the internet or other sources to research the cultural attitudes which might affect the way business is done there. Ss then prepare a brief presentation on their findings for the next lesson.

Building international teams Ex ❷:

Sample answer: *(230 words)*

Dear Jacek

Further to our conversation of 11 November, I am writing to confirm your visit. Since this will be your first trip to the United Kingdom, I include some information about the way we operate.

The first meeting is scheduled for 11.15 am and you should be ready to start promptly. Some people say that the British have a rather relaxed attitude to time and that starting fifteen minutes late is normal. However, Jim Walsh, the Head of Sales, is extremely keen on punctuality, so do not be tempted to take any risks.

One difference between this office and yours that you may notice is the apparent lack of formality between colleagues here. In Britain it is usual to use a person's first name once you have been introduced and you will usually be invited to do so. Also, please do not be offended if our staff here do not use your professional title; only medical doctors are given the title 'Doctor' here. As I said, especially between colleagues, it is common simply to use a person's first name.

A number of our managers are women and you should be aware that they are treated in exactly the same way as their male counterparts.

If you have any further questions, please do not hesitate to contact me on 020 779 2603.

I look forward to seeing you on 8 December.

Yours sincerely

Unit 7a Industrial espionage

Objectives:	To enable Ss to talk about information security
	To practise reading to identify the structure of a text
	To practise listening for gist and specific information
	To practise a collaborative speaking task
	To review asking for clarification
	To review conditionals 1 (real) and 2 (hypothetical)
Materials needed:	Cards **six cards; one set of cards per pair to be photocopied**

Unit overview

- **Research or espionage?**

Speaking	Ss discuss ways of accessing information about a competitor.
Reading	Ss read a jumbled article to find examples of industrial espionage.
	Ss put the paragraphs in the correct order.
Speaking	Ss discuss what measures their company takes to protect itself from industrial espionage.

- **Information security**

Listening 1	Ss listen to the start of a meeting and identify the problem.
Listening 2	Ss listen to the rest of the discussion and note down the action discussed and the implications of this action.
Language	Ss focus on conditionals 1 (real) and 2 (hypothetical).
	Ss focus on asking for clarification.
Speaking	Ss discuss a new information policy for a company using instructions on cards (*Speaking Test Part Three*).

Research or espionage?

1 **Ex ❶:** T asks Ss how a company can find out information about its competitors. T then asks Ss which of the methods they think are ethically acceptable.

> *Suggested answer:*
> *reading about the company in the newspapers, watching TV, looking at internet information, talking to people who work for the company, posing as a potential customer, stealing information, getting hold of product samples, spying, infiltration, hacking into the computer system*

2 **Ex ❷:** Ss read the article and find what methods of accessing information are mentioned.

> *stealing a sample of the product for analysis, bugging, infiltration, hacking, copying information onto a disk and taking it home, leaking inside information, photocopying internal documents*

3 **Ex ❸:** Ss read the article again and put the paragraphs into the correct order. When checking the answers, T asks Ss to identify the parts of the text which helped them.

> *1 C   2 G   3 A   4 J   5 D   6 H   7 B   8 F   9 I   10 E*

4 **Ex ❹:** Ss discuss the reasons for espionage.

5 **Ex ❺:** Ss discuss how their own company could reduce the risk of industrial espionage. Encourage them to think about their answers to the previous question.

> *Suggested answer:*
> *increase staff motivation, improve background checks on new staff, encourage staff to take the risk of espionage seriously, reduce the number of staff with access to sensitive data, 'anti-espionage plan' – remove computers with sensitive data from the company intranet*

Information security

6 **Ex ❶:** T explains that this exercise does not resemble an exam task; however it provides useful practice in listening for gist. Ss listen and identify the problem.

(1.31)

> *Suggested answer:*
> *Octacon has lost several important contracts to its rival, Centronics. Centronics seemed to know when the contracts were up for renewal and had information about Octacon's terms and conditions. Octacon needs to find out if one of its staff has leaked the information or if the company has been infiltrated.*

7   **Ex ❷:** Ss listen to the rest of the discussion and complete the table.

Action	Implications
Check CVs and previous employers of everyone who has joined the company over the last twelve months.	It will take ages.
Check appraisal records for anyone in Sales who is unhappy.	They need to be thorough. If they don't find anything in Sales, they need to check appraisal records for the whole company.
Check who's got access to what information.	
Issue individual computer passwords.	The company would know who was logging on, when and what they were looking at.
Check employees' email.	The company could see who was dissatisfied and then check their appraisal notes. But it would be bad for morale if anyone found out.
Bring in a security consultant to pose as a temp in the Sales Department.	She could find out all the gossip. But again, it would be very bad for morale if anyone found out.

8   **Ex ❸:** T refers Ss to the example sentences. Ss then look through the audioscript to find further examples of conditional forms. Ss should be encouraged to categorise examples of the conditional forms rather than discuss each occurrence separately. T reminds Ss also to pick out examples where the conditional element may be implicit rather than explicit, e.g. *It wouldn't do much for morale either.* (See the end of this unit for further information on conditionals 1 (real) and 2 (hypothetical).)

Conditional 1 (real) and 2 (hypothetical) forms are bolded in T's audioscript.

9   **Ex ❹:** Ss read through the audioscript again and complete the **Don't forget!** section with phrases for asking for clarification. T should point out the importance of asking for clarification in the Speaking Test.

Listening 1:   *But surely, you don't think that ... ?*
Listening 2:   *Which means ..., right?*
        You don't think ..., do you?
        Do you mean ... ?

10 Ex ❺: This exercise practises the skills needed for Speaking Test Part Three. Ss establish a context and try to reach agreement on what information should be available to staff and the implications of the new policy. However, additionally in this case Ss use cards to practise giving, justifying and clarifying opinions and agreeing and disagreeing. Before the lesson, T should have photocopied cards from the back of the T's Book. T gives each S a set of cards. These cards give Ss instructions to follow during the exercise (e.g. give an opinion and justify it, ask for someone's opinion). Each S throws down a card as he/she does what is asked on it. T may wish to assess Ss' performance using the Collaborative Task section of the **Speaking Test Assessment Sheet** on page 83 of the Student's Book.

(!) T should ensure that the Assessment Sheet has been presented clearly to Ss. (See T's notes for the **How to succeed** section of **Exam focus: Speaking** for further information.)

Alternative activity

T may wish to use this exercise for a mini-meeting rather than a simple discussion. T may also wish to add a competitive element: the winner is the first person to complete the task having used all the cards.

Exam focus: Speaking Test Part Three

This is a collaborative task. Candidates are required to have a brief guided discussion in pairs or threes. They are given a task sheet which outlines a business situation and the points which need to be discussed and decided together. Candidates have 30 seconds to prepare individually for the discussion.

Candidates should start by establishing a context (e.g. the type of company they work for). They are expected to be able to initiate, respond and turn-take appropriately without intervention by the examiner. Candidates need to be aware that they are expected to move the discussion towards a decision rather than simply discuss various options.

Conditionals 1 (real) and 2 (hypothetical)

The uses of the conditional which appear in the audioscripts are as follows.

Conditional 1 (real)

- **To refer to the consequences of an action/situation which the speaker considers to be probable:**
  *If there genuinely **is** a problem, then we**'ll have** to find out whether Centronics has infiltrated us.*
  *What **if** we **don't come** up with anything, what **are** we **going to** do then?*
  *Well, start with Sales and then **keep** looking **if** you **don't find** anything.*

Conditional 2 (hypothetical)

- **To refer to the consequences of an action/situation which the speaker considers hypothetical or unlikely:**
  *If word **got** out about this, then whoever's doing it **would stop** and **destroy** the evidence.*
- **In polite instructions or requests:**
  *And **if** I **could see** them, too, I **could see** who's dissatisfied.*

Both these conditional forms can be used to refer to present or future time.

Conditional 1 (real) tends to be thought of as:

if + present simple	*will* + infinitive

However, most examples do not fit into this rigid pattern. It may be more useful for Ss to think of it as:

if + any present form	any modal (or *going to*) + infinitive

The imperative may also be used in the second clause.

Conditional 2 (hypothetical) tends to be thought of as:

if + past simple	*would* + infinitive

However, most examples do not fit into this rigid pattern. It may be more useful for Ss to think of it as:

if + past simple or continuous	certain modals + infinitive

T may wish to remind Ss that the conditional element of the sentence lies in the *if* clause; how the speaker views this element dictates the verb forms used in the sentence.

Ss should be aware that it is not always necessary to state both clauses; the conditional element is often understood implicitly rather than stated explicitly, e.g. *He**'d** never **agree** to those conditions.*

Unit 7b Business ethics

Objectives:	To enable Ss to talk about business ethics
	To practise reading for specific information
	To practise listening for gist and specific information
	To practise giving a short talk
	To review conditional 3 (hypothetical)

Unit overview

- ### What are business ethics?

Speaking	Ss discuss which of the three statements about ethics they agree with.
Reading	Ss read an extract from a report on ethics and identify the three most important features of an ethical organisation.
	Ss read the extract again and answer questions.
Language	Ss focus on formal report language and layout.
Speaking	Ss discuss the ethical issues they are most concerned about in their company.

- ### Ethical issues

Listening	Ss listen to five speakers talk about unethical conduct and decide what ethical issue is mentioned and the action taken by the company (*Listening Test Part Two*).
Speaking	Ss order the five cases in terms of their seriousness.
Language	Ss focus on past conditionals.
Speaking	Ss prepare and give a one-minute talk (*Speaking Test Part Two*).
Optional task	Ss use the internet to research a company accused of ethical misconduct and write a report on the scenario and their decisions.

What are business ethics?

1 **Warmer (books closed):** T asks Ss what they understand by the term *business ethics*.

2 **Ex ❶:** Ss read the statements and say which ones they agree with.

3 **Ex ❷:** Ss read the survey extract and say what the CEOs considered to be the three most important features of an ethical organisation. T may wish to point out to Ss that the answer can be found in the main body of the text rather than on the diagram.

 fair employment practices, legal compliance, delivery of high quality goods and services

4 **Ex ❸:** Ss read the survey again and decide if the four statements are true or false. When checking the answers, T asks Ss to identify where the answers appeared in the text.

> 1 *F – It was initially sent to 500 CEOs but the sample was then extended to include a further twenty executives in the public sector.*
> 2 *F – Corporate philanthropy was given the least weight when describing ethical organisations.*
> 3 *T – 38% of organisations protect whistle-blowers.*
> 4 *F – Security of information was the issue with which respondents were least satisfied.*

5 **Ex ❹:** Ss find examples of the points related to formal reports. This exercise is designed to focus Ss on features of formal reports which will help them in their writing. (See the end of this unit for further information on formal reports.)

> ***Report layout***
> *use of bullet points and visuals, not dense text*
>
> ***Formal vocabulary***
> *selected, in terms of, in response to, expressed, further, key findings, legal compliance, employment practices, corporate philanthropy, participating organisations, ethical or legal violations, to indicate, level of attention, of greatest concern, issue, respondents*
>
> ***Ellipsis***
> *In response to an increasing level of interest ~~which was~~ expressed ... , ... an increase of 22% ~~which was~~ reported ... , ... to indicate the level of attention each ~~issue~~ received ... , Of these issues, the two ~~issues which were~~ most frequently identified ...*
>
> ***Participles***
> ***selected*** *on the basis of size, an **increasing** level of interest **expressed**, **written** statements, **participating** organisations, an increase of the 22% **reported**, the two most frequently **identified***

6 **Ex ❺:** Ss discuss the ethical issues they are most concerned about in their company.

Ethical issues

7 **Ex ❶:** This exercise practises the skills needed for Listening Test Part Two. Ss listen to a set of five extracts twice and complete two tasks for each extract. T points out that for the first extract Ss should answer questions 1 and 6, for the second extract 2 and 7 etc. T asks Ss to read through the lists of ethical issues and consequences and think of words or phrases they would expect to hear connected with each one. For example, for *a manager was dismissed*, Ss might expect to hear words such as *sacked*, *fired*, *made redundant*. Ss then listen and match each speaker with an ethical issue and consequence.

1 F	2 C	3 A	4 H	5 D
6 P	7 I	8 N	9 K	10 M

> **Exam focus: Listening Test Part Two**
>
> Candidates listen to five short topic-related extracts and complete two tasks, which may involve identifying any combination of the following for each extract: speaker, topic, function, opinion or feelings. The five extracts are heard twice. Both tasks test candidates' ability to listen for gist and specific information.
>
> Candidates should be aware that each extract contains both a Task One answer and a Task Two answer. Some candidates may prefer to deal with Task One during the first listening and Task Two during the second listening, or they may choose to attempt the two tasks simultaneously. For each task, they have a list of eight options to choose from. Incorrect options are included in the recordings in order to distract unwary candidates.

8 **Ex ❷:** Ss work in pairs or small groups and put the five cases of unethical behaviour into order of seriousness. T points out to Ss that they should focus on the specific cases referred to and not the general concepts. Ss may need to listen to the audio CD again or look at the audioscript before doing this exercise. T may wish to ask Ss if they think the consequences of each action were just and whether the consequences would have been similar in their country.

9 **Ex ❸:** T refers Ss to the example sentences. Ss then read through the audioscript to find further examples of conditional forms. Ss should be encouraged to categorise examples of conditional forms rather than discuss each occurrence separately. (See the end of this unit for further information on Conditional 3 (hypothetical).)

> *Conditional forms are bolded in the audioscript.*

10 Ex ❹: This exercise practises the skills needed for Speaking Test Part Two. When setting up this task, T may wish to refer Ss to the framework for planning short talks on page 81 of the Student's Book. Ss take turns to make and listen to each other's short talks. Those listening should be encouraged to make notes and ask questions at the end. T may wish to ask Ss to use the Short Talk section of the **Speaking Test Assessment Sheet** on page 83 of the Student's Book to evaluate each other's performance. Before the lesson, T should have made photocopies of the Assessment Sheet for Ss to use. Once Ss have completed their own talks, play the audio CD which contains example models of each talk. (See T's notes for Exam focus: Speaking for further information for suggestions on how to use the models.)

(!) T should ensure that the Assessment Sheet has been presented clearly to Ss. (See T's notes for the **How to succeed** section of **Exam focus: Speaking** for further information.)

Exam focus: Speaking Test Part Two

Each candidate chooses a topic from a list of three options (one general, one general business and one specialised business topic) and speaks about it for one minute. To avoid overlap, the candidates receive different lists. When each candidate has finished speaking, the other candidate has an opportunity to ask one or two questions. Candidates can take notes during their partner's presentations.

Candidates have one minute to think about what they want to say and should use the time to make notes. Ss are expected to plan, organise and present their ideas clearly. They should use appropriate phrases to structure their talk.

This exercise differs from the exam in that there are only two topics to choose from. In the exam itself candidates choose from three options.

---

11 The newspaper headlines are for visual effect rather than being an integral part of the unit. However, T may wish to ask Ss briefly to discuss the newspaper headlines in relation to the situation in their own company and country.

12 Ex ❺: Once again, the Optional Task links the lesson with the outside world. This exercise practises the skills needed for Writing Test Part Two.

Formal reports

Formal reports may contain the following features.

Report layout
See T's notes at the end of **Exam focus: Writing**.

Formal vocabulary
See Ts' notes at the end of Unit 5a.

Ellipsis
See Ts' notes at the end of **Exam focus: Writing**. Ellipsis is particularly common in passives and relative clauses, e.g. *The matter* which was *discussed at the meeting has now been addressed.*

Participles
Past participles are a feature of ellipsis in passives, e.g. *the issues identified*. Past participles are also used adjectivally, e.g. *spoken language*. Present participles are used in a type of ellipsis where the *-ing* form replaces a relative clause, e.g. *the people who attended/the people attending*.

Conditional 3 (hypothetical)

The uses of the conditional which appear in the audioscripts are as follows.

Reporting
- **To report a future conditional:**
  *She went straight to the board and warned them that she**'d take** legal action **if** nothing **was done** about it.*

Conditional 3 (hypothetical)
- **To refer to the hypothetical consequences of an action which did not take place:**
  ***If** you**'d looked** around the workplace, I guess you **would have seen** the evidence.*

Conditional 3 (hypothetical) tends to be thought of as:

if + past perfect	*would have* + past participle

However, it may be more useful for Ss to think of it as:

if + past perfect simple or continuous	any 'past' modal + *have* + past participle

Ss should be aware that it is not always necessary to state both clauses; the conditional element is often understood implicitly rather than stated explicitly, e.g. *Then he**'d have managed** to negotiate better terms.*

Unit 8a Global brands

Objectives:	To enable Ss to talk about global brands
	To practise reading for specific information
	To practise giving a short talk
	To practise report writing
	To review inversion

Unit overview

- **Making brands global**

Speaking	Ss discuss the foreign brands they buy and why.
	Ss complete a table with names of companies and industries.
	Ss discuss aspects of famous brands which they think are global.
Reading	Ss read an article about global brands and answer multiple-choice comprehension questions (*Reading Test Part Three*).
Language	Ss focus on inversion.
Speaking	Ss discuss global brands from their country which are based on cultural stereotypes.

- **Promoting a brand**

Speaking	Ss say whether they have bought one of six famous brands and why.
	Ss discuss how one of these brands is promoted in their country and then give a brief summary of their ideas.
	Ss prepare and give a one-minute talk (*Speaking Test Part Two*).
Writing	Ss write a report about how a brand could be globalised (*Writing Test Part Two*).
Optional task	Ss visit the Ford website and prepare a short presentation on the company's brands and markets.

Making brands global

1 **Ex ❶**: Ss discuss briefly what foreign brands they buy and why.

2 **Ex ❷**: Ss complete the table with the brands and industries. T may wish to point out that a 'diversified' company is involved in a number of sectors. Ss should complete the information about the companies they know first and then finish the exercise by a process of elimination.

World's top 10 brands by value, 2010

	Brand name	Origin	Industry	Value ($m)
1	**Coca-Cola**	*USA*	*Beverages*	*70,452*
2	*IBM*	*USA*	**Computers**	*64,727*
3	**Microsoft**	*USA*	*Software*	*60,895*
4	*Google*	*USA*	**Internet service**	*43,557*
5	*General Electric*	*USA*	**Diversified**	*42,808*
6	**McDonald's**	*USA*	*Food*	*33,578*
7	*Intel*	*USA*	**Semiconductors**	*32,015*
8	**Nokia**	*Finland*	*Telecoms*	*29,495*
9	*Disney*	*USA*	**Entertainment**	*28,731*
10	**Hewlett-Packard**	*USA*	*IT*	*26,867*

3 **Ex ❸**: Ss look at the three aspects of a brand and decide which aspects of the brands listed are global. T may wish to illustrate what is meant by the aspects. McDonald's, for example, uses the same concept in each country; the products are virtually identical (even though McDonald's adapts its range slightly to suit local markets, e.g. by introducing salads in certain countries); the McDonald's name, trademark, symbols and logo are the same everywhere (even though names of products may differ slightly). Ss then read the article and compare their answers.

Coca-Cola: *globalises all three aspects.*
Mars: *has global products and a global logo but different concepts are associated with the chocolate bar.*
Hertz: *globalises all three aspects.*
Nike: *globalises all three aspects.*
Barilla: *globalises all three aspects.*
Nescafé: *has a global concept and a global logo but different products to suit local tastes.*

4 **Ex ❹:** This exercise practises the skills needed for Reading Test Part Three. T asks Ss to read through the questions. Ss then read the text again in more detail to answer the questions and complete the sentences.

> 1 B   2 D   3 A   4 B   5 C   6 C

> **Exam focus: Reading Test Part Three**
>
> Candidates read a 500–600 word text and answer six multiple-choice questions. This tests ability to read for specific information.
>
> Candidates read the whole text briefly for general understanding and then read the questions and options. Ss re-read the text and answer the questions they feel sure of. They then concentrate on scanning the text for the answers to the remaining questions. The questions follow the order of the text, which should help Ss narrow down the location of a relevant passage in the text.

5 **Ex ❺:** T refers Ss to the example sentence. T asks Ss what they notice about the word order. Ss then read through the article to find further examples of inversion and discuss how it is used. T may wish to point out that the examples all appear in the first column of text. (See the end of this unit for further information on inversion.)

> *Rarely, though, **is it** realistic and profitable to extend all of them. (Para. 2)*
> ***Nowhere is globalisation** more desirable than in sectors that revolve around mobility. (Para. 3)*

6 **Ex ❻:** Ss think of a brand from their country which makes use of cultural stereotypes and discuss the values associated with these stereotypes. T may wish to give an example, e.g. the BBC makes use of the British stereotypes of impartiality, high quality and authority throughout the world.

Promoting a brand

7 **Ex ❶:** Ss discuss briefly whether they have bought products from any of the companies shown and give the reasoning behind their choices.

8 **Ex ❷:** Ss choose one of the companies and consider each of the points on the diagram in relation to how the company promotes the brand in their country. T then asks one S per group to summarise their ideas informally.

9 **Ex ❸:** This exercise practises the skills needed for Speaking Test Part Two. When setting up this task, T may wish to refer Ss to the framework for planning short talks on page 81 of the Student's Book. Ss take turns to make and listen to each other's short talks. Those listening should be encouraged to make notes and ask questions at the end. T may wish to ask Ss to use the Short Talk section of the **Speaking Test Assessment Sheet** on page 83 of the Student's Book to evaluate each other's performance. Before the lesson, T should have made photocopies of the Assessment Sheet for Ss to use. Once Ss have completed their own talks, play the audio CD which contains example models of each talk. (See T's notes for Exam focus: Speaking for further information for suggestions on how to use the models.)

> **Exam focus: Speaking Test Part Two**
>
> Each candidate chooses a topic from a list of three options (one general, one general business and one specialised business topic) and speaks about it for one minute. To avoid overlap, the candidates receive different lists. When each candidate has finished speaking, the other candidate has an opportunity to ask one or two questions. Candidates can take notes during their partner's presentations.
>
> Candidates have one minute to think about what they want to say and should use the time to make notes. Ss are expected to plan, organise and present their ideas clearly. They should use appropriate phrases to structure their talk.

10 **Ex ❹:** This exercise practises the skills needed for Writing Test Part Two. T may wish to ask Ss to prepare a detailed plan in class showing how they intend to organise their ideas before they write a proposal for homework. When setting up this task, T reminds Ss that the language used in proposals is very similar to the language used in reports and may wish to refer Ss back to Unit 1a, Exam focus: Writing (page 77 of the Student's Book) for useful report language and Units 5a and 7b, which look at features of formal reports. If Ss do the writing task in class, T may wish to ask Ss to exchange proposals and give each other feedback using the **Writing Test Assessment Sheet** on page 78 of the Student's Book. Before the lesson, T should have made photocopies of the Assessment Sheet for Ss to use. (See the end of this unit for a sample proposal.)

> **Exam focus: Writing Test Part Two (Report)**
>
> For Writing Test Part Two, candidates write a 200–250 word proposal, piece of business correspondence or report. All the points in the rubric must be included in the answer. To generate the range of language required at this level, the task input is broad and non-specific, which means that a reasonably high background knowledge is needed by the candidate. To ensure that no candidate is disadvantaged a choice of tasks is given. The task tests the ability to produce an appropriate piece of extended directed writing.
>
> For the proposal, candidates are expected to plan, organise and present their ideas clearly. Proposals should be clearly set out, with paragraphs, headings (e.g. *Introduction, Findings, Conclusion*) and bullet points where appropriate. All proposals are expected to have a title.

11 **Ex ❺:** Once again, this Optional Task links the lesson with the outside world. Ss visit the Ford website and prepare a short presentation on the company's brands and markets.

Inversion

Inversion of the verb and subject may be used in both formal spoken and written English when the speaker's/writer's emphasis is on the word or phrase at the beginning of the sentence.

If the sentence contains an auxiliary verb, it comes before the subject.
e.g.   *Never **has** this been more apparent than with the takeover of MLM.*
If there is no auxiliary, *do*, *does*, or *did* is added.
e.g.   *Not only **does** it increase turnover but it also results in economies of scale.*

The words or phrases followed by inversion often have a limiting or negative meaning.
e.g.   ***Nowhere** is globalisation more desirable than in sectors revolving around mobility.*
        ***Rarely** is it realistic to extend all aspects of a brand.*

Inversion may also occur after *as*.
e.g.   *Our Baltic centre has shown continued growth, **as** have our Mediterranean centres.*

Inversion can be used in formal writing to replace *if* in conditional clauses.
e.g.   ***Had we been** aware of the situation ...*

Promoting a brand Ex ❹:

Sample answer: *(249 words)*

Introduction

This proposal sets out to examine options for the successful globalisation of our 'Borders' brand. The initial market under consideration is Continental Europe. For the purposes of this proposal, we will be considering three aspects of the brand, namely our logo, the 'Borders' concept and finally, the product itself, 'Borders' wellington boots.

Findings

The following points summarise our key findings.
- *It was found that our existing logo, a pair of wellington boots encircled by the word 'Borders', is visual enough to be used in markets where English is not widely spoken.*
- *Attitudes to outerwear differ throughout Europe and our boots are likely to appeal to different market sectors in different countries. This has serious implications for the benefits we wish to publicise. Although Danish farmers would be willing to purchase such a high quality product, farmers in some countries would be unlikely to choose a British brand over a domestic product. However, the very Britishness of the product would appeal to the style-conscious elements of the French and Italian markets, summoning up images of the English upper classes and country houses.*
- *Our current product is multi-purpose and as such would not need adapting to suit different sectors of the European market.*

Conclusions

It was agreed that although the present logo and product are suitable for globalisation as they stand, we propose that the 'Borders' concept be adapted for different markets.

Recommendations

We recommend that further studies be carried out into the marketing strategies best suited to different European regions.

Unit 8b Global sourcing

Objectives:	To enable Ss to talk about suppliers
	To practise reading and listening for specific information
	To practise a collaborative speaking task
	To practise report writing
Materials needed:	Cards **six cards; one set of cards per pair to be photocopied**

Unit overview

- **Choosing a supplier**

  Speaking — Ss discuss the types of supplier their company uses and its criteria for choosing a supplier.

  Ss match the measurements with supplier performance criteria.

  Ss discuss the strengths and weaknesses of suppliers to their company.

- **Supplier relationships**

  Listening — Ss listen to an interview about supplier relationships and answer multiple-choice comprehension questions (*Listening Test Part Three*).

  Speaking — Ss recommend supplier relationships for three companies and say whether they could source globally.

- **Global sourcing**

  Reading — Ss read five supplier profiles and match the statements with the profiles (*Reading Test Part One*).

  Speaking — Ss decide which of the five suppliers would be most suitable for a European clothing company (*Speaking Test Part Three*).

  Writing — Ss write a report based on their decision (*Writing Test Part Two*).

Choosing a supplier

1 **Ex ❶:** Ss discuss briefly what type of suppliers their company uses and its criteria for choosing them. T may wish to point out that suppliers include not only providers of materials needed for production but also providers of services such as computer support. Most companies are also likely to need supplies of stationery and refreshments (e.g. for coffee and snack dispensers).

2 **Ex ❷:** Ss complete the table with the measurements. T may wish to point out that *warranty dollars* refers to the amount of money spent repairing or replacing sub-standard goods or services when they are under warranty.

Main criteria when choosing a supplier

Criteria	Definitions	Measurements
Cost	Cost relative to our competitors	**$ per unit**
Quality	Conformance to standards	*Per cent defective*
	Performance	**Satisfaction surveys**
	Reliability	**Warranty dollars spent**
Delivery	Speed	**Time to market**
	Reliability	**Total number of days late**
Flexibility	Product range	**Number of items in the catalogue**
	New product introduction	**Number of new product launches a year**

3 **Ex ❸:** Ss discuss the strengths and weaknesses of a supplier to their company.

Supplier relationships

4 **Ex ❶:** This exercise practises the skills needed for Listening Test Part Three. T asks Ss to read through the questions before listening. When checking the answers, T may wish to ask Ss to identify where the answers appeared in the audioscript.

1 C	2 B	3 A	4 B
5 B	6 C	7 A	8 C

Exam focus: Listening Test Part Three

Candidates listen to a 3–4 minute recording of two or three speakers and answer eight multiple-choice questions. The recording is heard twice. This task tests ability to listen for specific information.

The questions follow the order of the recording and are clearly signposted by the speaker(s). Incorrect options are included in the recording in order to distract unwary candidates.

---

5 **Ex ❷:** Ss discuss the most suitable supplier relationship for each situation.

> *Suggested answer:*
>
> **Car manufacturer**
> *Some kind of strategic alliance would be sensible here as the company might need to develop the brake system in conjunction with the supplier. Quality and responsiveness are likely to be key criteria. Some car companies even go so far as to integrate certain suppliers into their own factories. Car companies do have relationships with overseas suppliers; however, the speed and reliability of deliveries might be an issue.*
>
> **Toy company**
> *It would probably be logical to source the dolls globally as they are a commodity product and price would be the deciding factor. It would not be logical to enter into any long-term relationship with the supplier as the company would want to be free to choose on the basis of price.*
>
> **Restaurant**
> *Any decision as to a supplier would depend on the restaurant. Most restaurants buy locally. They probably do not enter into strategic relationships with suppliers so that they are free to shop around on the basis of quality, freshness, seasonal availability and price. However, large food chains (e.g. McDonalds) buy staple foods from key suppliers to ensure standardisation of quality throughout the world.*

Global sourcing

6 **Ex ❶:** This exercise practises the skills needed for Reading Test Part One. Ss read the texts and statements and match each statement with a company. Ss should be encouraged to pay attention to the use of qualifiers (*relatively, expensive* etc.). T then asks Ss to award a rating for *price, quality, delivery* and *flexibility* for each company – five being the highest and one the lowest score.

1	Hai Xin	2	Consort	3	Samokovska	4	Namlong
5	Shiva	6	Consort	7	Shiva	8	Samokovska

Suggested answer:

Consort	Price 5	Quality 2	Delivery 3	Flexibility 3
Samokovska	Price 2	Quality 5	Delivery 4	Flexibility 2
Namlong	Price 2	Quality 3	Delivery 5	Flexibility 3
Shiva	Price 4	Quality 4	Delivery 2	Flexibility 3
Hai Xin	Price 3	Quality 3	Delivery 3	Flexibility 4

(!) Ss need to be careful about the rating they give for price. A high price is negative; therefore, a low rating should be given for a high price – and vice versa.

Exam focus: Reading Test Part One

Candidates read a single text or five short related texts and eight statements. Ss then match each statement with the text it refers to. This tests ability to read for gist and global meaning.

Candidates should check that each text has been matched with only one statement.

---

7   **Ex ❷**: This exercise practises the skills needed for Speaking Test Part Three. Ss establish a context and try to reach agreement on the key criteria for suppliers and the most suitable supplier. T may wish to assess Ss' performance using the Collaborative Task section of the **Speaking Test Assessment Sheet** on page 83 of the Student's Book.

Alternative activity

T may wish to use this exercise for a mini-meeting. Before the lesson, T should have photocopied cards from the back of the T's Book. T gives each S a role-card describing the speaker's vested interest. Ss should behave in accordance with the information on their cards (without revealing it to the other Ss). After the meeting, Ss guess the vested interests of the other speakers.

Exam focus: Speaking Test Part Three

This is a collaborative task. Candidates are required to have a brief guided discussion in pairs or threes. They are given a task sheet which outlines a business situation and the points which need to be discussed and decided together. Candidates have 30 seconds to prepare individually for the discussion.

Candidates should start by establishing a context (e.g. the type of company they work for). They are expected to be able to initiate, respond and turn-take appropriately without intervention by the examiner. Candidates need to be aware that they are expected to move the discussion towards a decision rather than simply discuss various options.

---

8   **Ex ❸**: This exercise practises the skills needed for Writing Test Part Two. T may wish to ask Ss to prepare a detailed plan in class showing how they intend to organise their ideas before they write a report for homework. When setting up this task, T may wish to refer Ss back to Unit 1a and Exam focus: Writing (page 77 of the Student's Book) for useful report phrases and Units 5a and 7b, which look at features of formal reports. (See the end of this unit for a sample report.)

Exam focus: Writing Test Part Two (Report)

For Writing Test Part Two, candidates write a 200–250 word proposal, piece of business correspondence or report. All the points in the rubric must be included in the answer. To generate the range of language required at this level, the task input is broad and non-specific, which means that a reasonably high background knowledge is needed by the candidate. To ensure that no candidate is disadvantaged a choice of tasks is given. The task tests the ability to produce an appropriate piece of extended directed writing.

For the report, candidates are expected to plan, organise and present their ideas clearly. Reports should be clearly set out, with paragraphs, headings (e.g. *Introduction*, *Findings*, *Conclusion*) and bullet points where appropriate. All reports are expected to have a title.

Supplier relationships Ex ❸:

> *Sample answer:*   (246 words)
>
> *Introduction*
>
> *The aim of this report is to recommend a supplier for our new range of leisurewear. A committee from the Purchasing Department was presented with a shortlist of five potential suppliers to select from. The criteria considered were price, quality, delivery, and flexibility.*
>
> *Findings*
>
> *It was found that, taking the companies' overall ratings into consideration, there was negligible difference between suppliers. Consequently, the committee decided to narrow their focus to the areas considered to be of major importance for QuayWest's image, namely quality and price.*
>
> **Consort Trading**   *Despite offering the best deal financially, the company is unable to guarantee garments compliant with EU standards.*
>
> *Samokovska*   *Although it produces goods of an extremely high quality for exclusive markets, this supplier charges high prices, part of which would necessarily be passed on to customers.*
>
> **Namlong Sportswear**   *The poor standards of craftsmanship make it difficult to justify paying the prices quoted.*
>
> **Shiva Trading**   *Sample items from this supplier show an acceptable quality level. Furthermore, the deals currently on offer make it an attractive option.*
>
> **Hai Xin Group**   *There is some doubt as to whether garments produced by this company would meet EU standards. In view of this, the prices appear unreasonably high.*
>
> *Conclusion*
>
> *It was felt to be unwise to risk compromising the company's image by using suppliers of low quality goods. Similarly, using an expensive supplier could affect QuayWest's reputation for value for money.*
>
> *Recommendations*
>
> *Consequently, it is suggested that QuayWest negotiates a contract with Shiva Trading.*

Audioscripts

Unit 1a: Work roles

Listening  1.01–1.05

I've just moved from a company with a very strict hierarchy to a fastgrowing software company and it's been hard coming to terms with the changes. I **mean**, don't get me wrong, I **enjoy** my new job a lot more. I **have** a lot more responsibility now and everything's **done** in project teams and managed by objectives. The one thing I **do miss**, however, **is** that now, once a project's **running**, the team's pretty much on its own and **left** to solve any problems by itself. Before, there was always a superior I could turn to for help, and to be honest, I'd be much happier if that were still the case. Especially when you**'re starting** a new job, having someone to talk to can make things a lot easier.

I **produce** technical documents, you **know**, users' manuals and that sort of thing – nothing creative, **I'm** afraid. Our team's responsible for its own work schedules. And as long as everything's **finished** before the machine's **shipped**, it's up to us when we **do** it. So you'd think with e-mail and everything, we'd all be able to work from home or come and go as we **please** – but that's not the case. Unfortunately, it's a very conservative company so everyone's still **clocking** in and out at the same time. I **suppose** the managers have always worked a routine nine to five and just **can't** imagine anything else being possible.

I'm an IT consultant and I'm **working** for a small leisure group on a oneyear contract. So I'm **travelling** around Europe a lot, which I **know** **sounds** very glamorous, but it's just a case of jetting in, fixing a hotel's computer and then jetting out again. It also **means** I'm on call and work very ... shall we **say** 'flexible' hours, including many weekends. Oh and I'm also responsible for the website, which I **work** on from home. What I **miss** **is** support from colleagues, you **know**, being able to discuss problems or things like the latest technology with other IT professionals in the same job. So, yes, it**'s** definitely the social side of my job I'd like to improve.

Well, I'm a temp and I'm **working** as a PA for a law firm in London just now. It's a medium-sized firm that's grown quickly so its organisation **is** very much like that of a smaller company. OK, I **know** it's unreasonable to expect a definite job description – I **mean**, if something **needs** doing, then I **think** whoever's available should do it. But I'm already responsible for managing the diaries and correspondence of two senior managers, so when the telephone's **ringing** all day and people **keep** asking me to photocopy reports or even make them coffee, it just **becomes** impossible to get anything done.

I **work** for the UK subsidiary of a Japanese company and it's very Japanese in terms of the way it's run. I've just got a new boss, who's come over from Japan. We **seem** to be getting on pretty well at the moment – he always **has** time for me and **gives** me lots of support. The only thing **is,** I **don't** really have a huge say in what I **do** – which **is** all right but sometimes it would be nice to be able to show a bit of initiative. Our work processes **are** totally standardised as fixed routines, which I **don't mind**. It's just that I always **have to** consult him before I **can** make even the smallest alteration to any job of any sort.

Unit 1b: Company structure

Listening 1.06

I = Interviewer   D = Don

I So, what effect do you expect the change to retirement age to have on businesses?

D Well, we **have had** a reasonable degree of flexibility in retirement age for a long time now. Several years ago we **changed** our company policy so that employees could stay on at work beyond the age of 65, if they **were** men or 60 for women, as long as the employer **agreed** that they could. Some people, of course, choose to retire and others prefer to take retirement earlier. So, in one sense, these changes are likely to have little effect. Those people who want to continue working will probably do so. Those who wish to retire will. Where it affects businesses is in the administration of people's retirement, and in cases where an employee wants to continue working, but the employer thinks otherwise.

I And how many people do you think this will affect?

D It is difficult to put an exact figure on it. Our research **showed** that the overwhelming majority of requests to continue working were accepted: 81 per cent of them to be precise. So it is only in a minority of cases that someone will want to continue working, but the company would prefer for them not to. It's in these cases where we will have to find new roles or new responsibilities.

I Will this have any impact on company structure, do you think?

D This is where the difficulty lies, and where companies are most likely to encounter problems. We already have an aging working population, and younger employees are not getting the opportunities in their careers.

I You mean they are being passed over for promotion?

D It's more than that; it's a matter of younger employees getting the experience they need to succeed their elders when they eventually give way and retire. In a tight labour market, any company would want to retain highly skilled and experienced staff. And in many ways it makes sense for them to keep senior, more experienced people on for longer, even beyond retirement age, if they can. However, this means that staff **have been missing out** on gaining the experience that their older colleagues have. What you have is a company that is top heavy in people in their 60s or even 70s. This, in turn means that people in their 30s or 40s **have been looking** elsewhere for the career development that they require.

I And how is that likely to impact on the culture of companies?

D Naturally, every different company will deal with this problem in their own way. I expect that most will find a pretty similar solution. One way forward is for companies to retain people beyond the age of 65, but in a role which will encourage development of expertise. We **started looking** at this as a possible solution last year.

I You mean companies are likely to redeploy experienced people in a training role?

D I don't think it will be as formal as that – I'm not talking about specific training for people who already have the skills that enable them to do their jobs well. I would expect more experienced people working alongside younger staff, in a mentoring role, passing on the kind knowledge that can only come from experience. One can imagine, for example, an experienced engineer working alongside a younger colleague. The training that **has already started** is proving to be successful as older engineers **have been** gradually **handing over** decision making to their younger colleagues.

I Then you don't see older employees taking on new roles or adapting to changes in the company?

D I wouldn't say that. I can't see any reason why older staff shouldn't be able to adapt. There **has been** some **reluctance** on the part of individuals. I see this as a personal, rather than an employment problem. We see it as a staff solution to a problem, rather than a division among our employees. Change is something that affects all of us, experienced people as well as newer people.

I And how about in the workplace? How do you help older workers to take new ideas on board?

D I think this is the greatest challenge that employers face and is where the greatest benefits will be found. One thing that all businesses, large, small and medium-sized will have to do is to accept that the workforce dynamic will change. In my company and many others like it – competitors and those operating in other market sectors as well as in other industries – we are looking for ways of making greater use of the increased diversity that will come into the workforce. We have to develop teams of workers on the shop floor, for example, where we look to the balance of youth and experience. **We have already developed** teams where younger staff have more formal qualifications and older people have greater experience.

I And how **have** people **adapted** to working in these teams?

D Very well, on the whole. We had expected managers and team leaders to take on the responsibility of resolving conflict and building mutual respect. What we've **found** is that this **has happened** organically, with hardly any intervention from outside the teams. People **accepted** the changes quite readily and **learned** new skills from each other. There is an increased dynamism that **has** **developed**. The young **have been acquiring** the working habits of their older colleagues. Absenteeism **has decreased** and new ideas and practices are becoming more easily accepted. I think this **was** all because of how we **organised** people into teams. Out first thought **was** about the people, not the job or any implications for productivity. We **allowed** people to make their own decisions about how they **worked**, and our staff **made** good use of that opportunity.

I How do you see this developing in the future?

D What I hope we will be able to do is take what we **have learned** from this and adapt it to other changes in the workplace. We're moving into an era of increased flexibility in the workforce, with such things as teleworking and hot-desking becoming the norm. As long as we can encourage our people to work in diverse teams – not only age related, I'm thinking of multi-skilled teams as well – then I can see teams operating as skill-sharing units within the company. I believe this can only be good for motivation and so for productivity, too. I think this is the challenge we have to rise to in the future.

Unit 2a: Stocks and shares

Listening 1 1.07

R = Richard   K = Katie

R Now retail stocks. They were quite strong about a year ago, but they have been quite volatile recently. So the question is, has the financial crisis driven them down? Our retail correspondent Katie Johnson joins me in the studio. So, Katie, first of all what drove these prices up in the first place?

K Well, some of the news stories about increased growth and the competition for market share would have attracted some investors looking for a quick profit – but I think the real driving force has been the fact that demand has exceeded supply. It has always been thought that retailers would do well in bad as well as good times. And during the consumer boom of the last few years, there was a noticeable shift towards reliable stocks, and with few share offers and a general unwillingness to sell, prices rose.

R And this is all because retailers were seen as a safe investment?

K Generally speaking, yes. When consumers have money to spend, they spend it and retailers are only too happy to provide the luxury items they want.

R And what about good old profits? Did they match the performance of the share price?

K Well, that's the interesting thing. As more and more consumers were busily spending, so retailers' profits went up. Much of that profit was reinvested, back into the businesses, as retailers looked for increased share of what was thought to be an ever expanding market. Take Tesco, for example. They are probably the most successful of the food retailers over the last ten years or so. Then, they had about a 25 per cent share of the grocery market. Today it is more than 30 per cent.

R So everyone wants to invest in the bigger players in the game?

K There is another reason, too. As a retailer, Tesco have been around for a long time, and were a well known store throughout the UK, even before they came to dominate the marketplace. What is interesting is the change in its position in the market that Tesco has undergone. They were originally a shop where people went to buy food cheaply. Tesco's recent history has been one of expansion in the UK and overseas, and one of diversification. They now sell groceries alongside white goods, financial services and clothing, to name but a few. Other retailers have followed suit, but Tesco has led the way. Throughout the boom, it seemed that everything Tesco touched would turn to gold. Investors are always looking to a business they know, even if their position changes.

R As long as it remains successful, though?

K Naturally. Unless there is a return, the investors will look elsewhere.

R And grocery retailers have remained successful, haven't they?

K In the main, yes. The big fish have continued to lead the sector, but it hasn't been easy. Tesco, and the other leading chains came under pressure from new players, such as Lidl and Aldi. These retailers came in at the discount end of the market. And while their share remains relatively small, some two or three percent, they have made inroads into Tesco's share – that fell by half of one percent over the last couple of years.

R So, let's turn to the effect of the financial crisis. How has that affected the larger retailers?

K Well, the immediate effect on consumers was one that shook their confidence. We all saw the TV pictures of giant financial institutions going to the wall, of bank employees walking out of their offices with their personal effects in boxes and for a time none of us knew where it would end. This shock made people very uncertain, and they suddenly became much more careful with their disposable income. Confidence in the stock markets fell, too. We were due a sell-off of highly valued shares. Investors took their profits and looked for safer places taking a more long term view of what they were prepared to invest. Some of those profits went into the bond market, and some into precious metals.

R For many people the fall in share prices seems surprising. Recession or no recession, people still need to buy food. So, why did share prices fall?

K The simple answer is the usual one. Confidence. As I hinted at before, investors saw the overall falls following the bank collapses and moved to more long term investments. It's no accident that the price of gold has risen to record levels in recent months. Another reason is that the big grocers are no longer simply food retailers. Tesco, for example, sells 16 per cent of all microwave ovens in the UK and has significant interests in telecoms and insurance. When consumers are forced to tighten their belts, it's the large ticket items – the expensive goods – that are the first that they cut back on.

R So there is likely to be a downward trend in share price, then?

K Yes and no. There was an appreciable fall throughout the markets in the initial wake of the bank collapses; a rationalisation of the market as it appeared to be at the time. Then share prices levelled out, although there are still challenges that these companies need to face up to – from competitors and from changes in consumer spending. There are still profits to be made, still rises and falls depending on local conditions but in the short to medium term we can expect some stability, overall.

R OK, then Katie, here's the big question. What's the market going to do next?

K Oh, now, Richard, that's not easy to say with any certainty at all. The prices being paid will, inevitably, reflect the value of the company – as the market sees it, if not in real terms, and we are talking about high value businesses here. I can't see share prices falling for ever, and there is evidence that the prices have bottomed out and even begun to climb back. They are not yet at the levels they were at before the crisis, but moving in that direction. I think we can look forward to some interesting times. Once the discount sellers are better established in the market, they might think about repositioning themselves, just as Tesco did, and then the competition will regain some of its old edge. On the other hand, it may be that the market leaders will look to consolidate their core businesses, before going on to even bigger ventures. I think the wise investor can look forward to substantial returns, but they may take some time to be made.

Listening 2 1.08

R Now earlier you talked about Tesco, the UK's largest supermarket chain. And I understand you have a graph illustrating what's been happening to their share price over the last three months.

K Yes, and here it is. Now this is more or less typical of what's been happening throughout the sector for the last year, although Tesco being Tesco have been in a position to make themselves more attractive to investors than perhaps any of their competitors. The price had been reasonably stable at the end of last year. But as you can see, in the period immediately after Christmas there were some **fluctuations**. The price finally **recovered**, even reaching **a high** towards the end of February. But then the price fell and fell, even despite some small rises, due mainly to profit taking from investors, I think. So that, by the middle of March the price had **fallen** to a low of 378, from a high of 413 three weeks previously. It then finally rallied, getting back to just over the 405 mark in April. It fell slightly, before settling back to around the 395 that it is today.

R That's not another dip in consumer confidence bringing the price down from 413, is it?

K   No, I don't think so. We can expect **a dip** in spending in the months after Christmas, when not many of us have much spare cash to spend anyway. A fall in sales is fairly predictable at that time of year, and there's no suggestion of a price **collapse**. No, I think the reason is that those people who bought Tesco shares when they were round about 380 decided to take their profit and sell them once the price had reached 405 or thereabouts. If you had bought say 10,000 shares at £3.80 and sold them at £4.05, you would have made a tidy £2,500. Not bad for a month's investment.

Unit 2b: Mergers and acquisitions

Listening `1.09`

*Good morning. My name is Jason Labone and I work for Hinton and Bailey. We're an economic research consultancy, operating from the UK and we provide businesses with **economic forecasting** data. Today, I am here to say a little about what has been happening in mergers and acquisitions since the financial crisis of 2008. I will first look at why there has been something of an increase in the number of mergers in the last year or so and then move on to explain my view on how the recent **spate** of mergers differs from those that took place before the crisis and the downturn that resulted from that. Finally, I will say something of how I expect the future to develop, at least in the short to medium term. I hope to leave some time, at the end of the session for any questions or comments you may have, and perhaps we can end with some discussion of what businesses need to do to survive and to grow in the current economic circumstances.*

*So, why has there been an increase in the number of mergers, now that the financial sector has stabilised itself somewhat? One reason is that the recession the crisis provoked has led to a **fall in profitability** for many businesses in almost every industry. A further result of the recession has been that the market has changed, for many businesses. We have witnessed a sharp fall in customer confidence – spending is down and so are orders and companies are realising that **long-term growth** is hard to find. What's more, as a consequence of the financial crisis, share prices fell, and so a company's value has fallen, also. And while all this is going on, the financial institutions, and I am referring to the banks, here, have been rescued by governments. In many cases government has become the largest shareholder in these institutions. The banks are under pressure from government to generate finance to move the economy out of recession, and this is particularly so when the government is also a major shareholder.*

*Even in the financial sector itself, there has been a rash of mergers and the reasons behind these are typical of the reasons behind mergers in other sectors. Even before the financial crisis, small and medium-sized Building Societies had become less profitable. The larger players in the sector had issued shares and become banks. This enabled them to become **more competitive**, and in their attempts to maintain their profits, the smaller societies overstretched themselves in new, niche markets. This was made worse by the tightening of the property market after the crisis. Still further, as the economy started to rebuild, they were faced with the increased cost of increased financial regulation. The upshot is that there have been more than twelve mergers in this sector alone since the crisis of 2008. What we have seen in the industry is a **phase of re-organisation** in the face of new economic realities and this is a pattern we have seen, not only in other industries, but in other economies as well.*

*The question is, then, how is this surge in mergers different from those that occurred in the 1990s and again in the years before the financial crisis? I have already pointed out that the banks are under pressure, from government, to make finance available in order to help lead the economy out of recession. But nowadays, banks are behaving differently to the way they were before they were **bailed out**. Prior to 2008, banks were willing to take greater risks in search of profit, and it was this that helped to cause many institutions to get into trouble and some to fail. Banks are no longer willing to make 'bad' loans. However, acting conservatively, banks are making credit available, but only where it makes **good sense**, where it will assist businesses in an industry to grow securely.*

Let me give you an example; Kraft's takeover of Cadbury is typical of the current round of mergers. Before 2008, the most likely bid for Cadbury would have been from private equity, but this was not the case after the

*crisis. While the takeover was ongoing, there was talk of rival bids from **industry rivals**, such as Hershey and Nestlé. Incidentally, the same can be said for other recent mergers, too. This is reassuring for shareholders – and government is a shareholder these days. What reassures is that these mergers are seen as **more sustainable**, leading to long-term growth. Shareholders are pleased with the increase in value of their shares and government is happy that the industry is re-organising itself with an eye to the future. The financial institutions are able and prepared to finance deals like this because they see them as 'good' loans, enabling mergers which put the business in a better position to grow and make profit in the long term, guaranteeing that the debt will be repaid.*

*What then of the future? Well, we can't say that this is a trend that will continue forever, but for the present economic cycle the picture is more clear. With government as a shareholder we can expect to see the banks acting more and **more conservatively** in their lending. Gone are the days of the speculative takeover. We will see mergers and acquisitions funded at least partly by the banks, but with caution over the risks they are taking. We also expect to see, to a greater extent than before 2008, **bidders** using their own financial resources to fund mergers. Over the next few years, we shall see CEOs increasingly focused on maintaining a secure credit rating while looking for growth opportunities. At the same time, financial institutions will be looking at opportunities for less riskier, long-term credit. Having being bitten once by bad debt, the banks will want to ensure that their loans are repaid.*

Unit 3b: Entering a market

Listening `1.10`

*So, what's it like actually doing business with the Chinese? Well, it's difficult to describe because in China there's still no commonly shared perception of what's reasonable or normal in international business, so **standards and expectations** vary widely from place to place. That's why, when you're doing business in China, it's imperative that you do extensive **preparatory work**. This means finding out about the particular company, industry, city or region where you're doing business – and not just about the country as a whole.*

*One of the first things to remember is that the Chinese find it most discourteous if you are **late for meetings**. It may be, of course, that your first meeting will be in your hotel, but if not, then allow plenty of time for the journey as in most Chinese cities the **congestion** is every bit as bad as in London. A good tip is to take a business card with the company's address written in Chinese to show the taxi driver. When you get there, you will be greeted by your host, usually a **senior manager**, and probably some of his or her staff. The visitors will then be ushered into the meeting room.*

*The leader of your group will be expected to enter first and will generally be offered a seat beside the most senior Chinese person present. This person will usually chair the meeting and act as host and have a translator at his or her side. To begin with, all those present will swap **business cards**, in itself a very important ceremony, and there will be a short period of small talk. The host will then officially start proceedings with a '**brief introduction**' to the Chinese enterprise and its activities. The host may then invite the visiting team to speak. Now at this point it's appropriate for the UK side to begin to make its case. Don't forget to warn your host beforehand if you wish to include any **audio-visual aids** during this presentation. It's also extremely important that your team should be able to answer any questions on any aspect of your business proposal, your own company and your international competitors.*

*Following the meeting, the Chinese enterprise will probably arrange a **special dinner** for the UK guests. Small talk over dinner is essential for relationship-building. For most Chinese, the family counts above all else. It remains the dominant social and political unit in Chinese society so Chinese people will usually be very pleased to be asked about their **children** and their hopes for their children's future. In social relationships Chinese people almost always seek to preserve harmony and face. Hosts believe it is their duty to offer their visitors **hospitality**, even though the visitors themselves may much prefer a day off after intense negotiations. It's very common, for instance, for the host enterprise to organise* *sightseeing trips* for its guests and it would, of course, be a discourtesy not to accept these invitations.

Unit 4a: The future of work

Listening 🎧 ⟨1.11⟩

I = Interviewer   N = Neil

I   In the late 1990s, a small property company, Cottice Holdings, opened its first multi-occupant office building in the village of Aldbourne, about 50 miles to the west of London. As office buildings go, it wasn't an expensive project. Construction costs came to a little under two million pounds. It was, however, a project filled with risk. The developers had an idea, built the complex and waited for occupants. They were in the heart of the countryside, half an hour's drive from the motorway and access to the capital. So what was the thinking behind the project? We spoke to Cottice's MD, Neil Traynor.

N   It all started out as an idea sketched out on a napkin in a restaurant. Some friends and I, who were all self-employed professionals, lived locally and worked from home, were having one of our regular meals. We'd meet up about three or four times a year to chat and compare work – networking, really. Someone came up with an idea of having a space away from home with access to all the things we had in our home offices without moving to the big city. We knew what we wanted and where we wanted it, but had no idea of how we could do it.

I   What exactly did you want to do?

N   To find, or rather create, a good place where people would want to come and work. But, when we sat down and thought about it, we realised it needed to be more than that. Many self-employed people are pretty flexible by nature, and this meant we needed to provide them with a suitable working environment to reflect this. We started out with the idea of sharing offices between us, but for one reason or another that proved impossible. We decided to rent out office space to people in all sorts of industries. We looked at parking, the size of the offices, sharing communications and things like that. One important consideration was that there could be no hierarchy among the self-employed. Here, everyone is his or her own boss. So we don't have facilities like reserved parking or executive toilets.

I   So how is the building laid out?

N   It's centred around what we originally called the Resource Area. There's a kitchen with all the usual facilities, and next to it there was a room with a photocopier for the tenants to share. But in a relatively short space of time, we realised this was unnecessary. Technology had moved on and people were able to use their PCs to print copies of whatever they needed. What the tenants wanted was a space to sit, relax and look at the newspapers. So that's now a lounge area. We've recently added a TV, so people can catch up with the news that way, too. That's on the first floor, along with three of the smaller offices. Below that, on the ground floor, is the reception area and the two large offices. The top floor has five more offices. That makes ten in all. They're all connected by a central stairway. People tend to bump into each other in the corridors, and then socialise in the lounge.

I   So people meet by chance, rather than intentionally, then?

N   At first, yes. Remember the people in these offices don't work together. Each office is actually a separate business. What we've tried to create is an organic space for people to use as they wish; and I think we've succeeded in this. The lounge itself was established because the tenants asked for it. They wanted a place where they could sit and chat with other workers in the building. The reception area is an important focal point, too. We have a picture gallery of the tenants there. This helps to let them know who is a part of the office community, and it helps with security too. It's good for people to know who comes and goes from the building. The reception desk isn't staffed full time, and the tenants have begun to keep an eye on the area, informally throughout the day. Having a central rest area has really helped this community feeling to grow.

I   Do you think that these offices have made a difference to the way people work?

N   In some ways, yes. In others, no. Work is work and all our tenants are hard working, self-motivated people, who like to get on with things. However, they do find it easier to be more productive away from the home environment. They definitely step into 'work' when they arrive here. I also think that one thing self-employed people sometimes find difficult is the lack of day-to-day interaction with colleagues. People often use the lounge as a place to talk through ideas or problems, and they are generally doing this with a colleague who works in an entirely different field. It's changed the way we look at the office, too. We're planning another development, not too far from here. We're paying much more attention to how we can foster the sense of community that we enjoy here. What we've realised is that people need contact with the people they share a building with, just as much as they need the work that they do.

I   Even when your tenants are all self-employed in different fields?

N   Yes. There is an enormous amount of everybody's work which is similar to, or related to the work someone else in another field does. Among the people in this building are a couple of accountants, a designer and several people in financial services. We've also seen tenants whose businesses have outgrown these offices. The self-employed have become employers and have moved on to larger premises. Much of business is about networking, and I know that John, one of the accountants does some work for one of our former tenants who has moved on to bigger and better things. That's just one of the many contacts that have come from the shared workplace. We're looking into ways that we can connect our new site with this one, precisely for that reason. Contact, it seems, has become our selling point.

Unit 4b: e-business

Listening 🎧 ⟨1.12–1.16⟩

Well, it's already made a huge impact and by the time the project's fully implemented, we*'ll have networked* over 300,000 employees and suppliers – they'll all be able to communicate through e-mail. And it's this interconnectivity, it's changing everything about the way we work. I mean, last year around 15 per cent of our in-service staff development was carried out through Web-based distance learning using the company intranet. And we reckon that for every 1,000 days of classroom-based teaching that's supplied by distance learning, it generates about $500,000 in efficiency gains. And this year we*'ll be delivering* up to 30 per cent of our courses by distance learning. So we*'ll be looking* at savings of over $100 million.

We're one of the largest insurance organisations in Canada, offering a wide range of financial products. We rely on a system of independent agents to distribute our products so it's really important to maintain a close relationship with them. This used to be done over the telephone but that was all very time-consuming for our employees and meant we could only supply agents with information during office hours. Now we have the extranet, which means that all our representatives can keep in touch around the clock and get the latest information about offerings. They can also request back-up articles and information such as telemarketing scripts and advertisements. And of course, we*'ll be introducing* more and more new product lines so it's essential that our agents get the back-up they need.

We're one of the Netherlands' leading banks with 1,300 branches here and abroad. We deal with both businesses and consumers but our primary focus is small and medium-sized businesses – SMBs as we call them. As part of our offering to SMBs, we recently launched a Web-based euro project which provides free briefings to both customers and staff about the European currency. Since the issues surrounding the euro are constantly changing, people will need regular updating. By providing up-to-the-minute bulletins, we're establishing ourselves as a major player in the Eurozone countries. This, in turn, is enhancing our clients' perceptions of us and we*'ll be aiming to* strengthen and expand our customer base in the near future.

Well, we are one of France's most prestigious bicycle manufacturers, selling mainly to professionals and people with a real passion for cycling as a sport. The best bit about our new website is that it lets customers actually design their own personalised cyber cycle. All they have to do is choose a basic model and then decide what frame, wheels, pedals, colour and so on they want. They pay online by credit card and the bike is then delivered to their nearest dealer within 14 days. It's as simple as that. Our business was initially aimed at mostly French customers but with the new way of using the internet, we have been able to create an international presence at a fraction of what it would have cost to advertise outside the domestic market.

After recent restructuring we felt we needed to change the company culture to reflect our leaner structure. Processes that used to be highly bureaucratised needed to be simplified. One area we really had to tackle was procurement. After filling in massive amounts of paperwork, getting requisite signatures and then faxing orders off, our employees sometimes had to wait over a month for things like office material and PCs to get here. A real advantage with the new system is there's less margin for error because if the form isn't filled in correctly, then the system says so immediately. So less time'll be wasted on sorting out problems. By the end of the year we'**ll have reduced** our paper invoices from five million to zero.

Unit 4: Exam practice (Exam focus CD)

Listening Part One 2.01

Good morning and welcome to Eldertree Cosmetics. My name's Maria Darcy and I'm the Managing Director. I'm here today to tell you a little bit about the history of the company before you're taken on the official tour.

So, Eldertree Cosmetics was founded by Olivia Jenkins in **1975** originally under the name of Eldertree Cottage. And in those days it really was very much a cottage industry with Olivia and her husband Mike producing a range of natural soaps in their own kitchen. The soaps proved to be a recipe for success and sales took off due to the **popularity** of simple, chemical-free products. It soon became clear, though, that Olivia and Mike would be unable to satisfy demand if they continued working out of their kitchen. So in 1977 Mike began searching for **suitable premises** and this resulted in the move to the Old Bakery in the town centre.

At the start of the next decade sales continued to grow dramatically and Olivia and Mike widened their product range to enter new markets such as haircare and cosmetics. This led to **rapid expansion** and a change of name to Eldertree Cosmetics. It was at this point that Olivia and Mike realised they needed support with their sales and marketing efforts. So they took on an experienced Sales Manager, who was able to win **substantial contracts** with some of the largest UK cosmetics retailers.

This significant increase in business meant that Eldertree needed to recruit a lot more staff and upgrade its facilities. The company had reached a critical point. In order to develop, it required the **resources and knowledge** that only a large and established organisation could offer. And faced with several takeover bids, Olivia and Mike finally decided that in the interests of Eldertree and its employees, they would sell the company to the UK's biggest **high-street chemist**, Greenaway, which they did in 1987.

Greenaway's first move was to look at ways of increasing productivity. Although the Old Bakery site had been upgraded over the years, it was still limited by its size and layout. So in 1988 Greenaway began construction of the **new factory**, which was completed at the end of the following year. The other major decision which was taken at this time was to continue to trade under the Eldertree **brand name** and not that of its parent company.

Today Eldertree Cosmetics is a state-of-the-art producer of high-quality cosmetic products. Structural changes have seen certain functions move to Greenaway's Head Office. By moving its **marketing operations** to Greenaway, for example, Eldertree has not only cut costs, but also enjoyed the advantages of its parent's substantial advertising budget. And I'm sure you're all familiar with the new TV campaign. Despite the fact that Eldertree has grown enormously, it still retains a **family atmosphere**, with many of the original employees from the Old Bakery

still working for the company today. Over the last ten years or so, these loyal employees have seen the Eldertree name successfully establish itself as a **market leader** in both the UK and overseas.

On that note, I'd like to hand you over to Samantha Eagle, our PR Manager, who'll be conducting your tour of the factory today.

Part Two   2.02

Well, I guess on the whole it was quite interesting talking about setting and meeting objectives and co-ordinating projects. It's just that I'd hoped we'd learn more practical things like how to motivate groups and manage conflict and make group communication more effective. Anyway, I was pretty tired by the end of the day and I got in quite late because the centre was a long way from home. But that in itself wasn't really a problem. I think one day would have been more than enough. I didn't really understand why they needed two whole days. It wasn't that expensive though, so I'm hoping I'll be allowed to go on another course soon. There are some good writing skills courses around, I believe.

I feel a lot more confident now having done the course. The trainer gave us some really great tips on preparing more effectively. And I also got to see myself on video. There I was talking about our latest product when most of the time I was standing in front of the screen. So no-one in the audience could see my nice OHTs anyway. We certainly didn't have any complaints about the price even though it was pretty expensive. But I can't understand why they held it in Newcastle. It took me half the day to get there and I was exhausted before the course even started. We really should have found somewhere closer to the office.

I had a great time. We did lots of role-plays, mainly about delegating or dealing with interruptions, which I really enjoyed. And I think it must have done me some good. Even my boss has noticed that I'm getting better at prioritising my workload. And this week I managed to get my report in before the deadline for a change. There must have been about twenty of us by the time all the latecomers had arrived, which was about right for the group dynamics. The only thing that I'd change would be the refreshments. You'd have thought they could have provided more than just a salad for lunch, wouldn't you? It wasn't even particularly fresh either.

Originally, I'd wanted to do the effective negotiations course. But my boss told me this course would be more useful. You know what I'm like. Even when I don't want to do something, I end up saying 'yes'. Even now I still find it difficult to say 'no', but at least this course has made me more confident about trying to stick up for myself. We covered a lot of stuff. But of course you can't expect the trainer to do everything in just six sessions, can you? So we had to miss out on some really interesting topics. I was a bit disappointed, for example, that we didn't do anything on body language.

The programme itself looked really interesting, which is why I went for this course rather than the assertiveness training one. And I guess we did have a few useful topics like writing minutes and preparing agendas. And we started looking at roles, especially the role of the chairperson. But all in all, it was really disappointing and so chaotic. We never really knew what we were supposed to be doing. But then the tutor didn't seem to know either. She kept taking calls on her mobile during the sessions and I wouldn't be surprised if it was someone phoning her to tell her what to do next! Good job it didn't cost too much. Otherwise we'd have been asking the centre for our money back.

Part Three   2.03

S = Sue   P = Peter

S   And today on Business Spot we have the winner of the 'South-East Company of the year' award, Peter Jones, Manager of corporate travel agency Corporate Direct. Hello Peter. And congratulations on your award.

P   Thank you, Sue.

S   So, Peter, how has the award affected your company so far?

P   Well, Sue, we've been stunned by all the media attention, which might even generate some new business, you never know. But the real benefit is the boost to morale. Everyone's been working extremely hard to make the business a success and it's great to see their efforts rewarded.

S   So why did you start Corporate Direct?

P   Well, about six years ago I was made redundant. I couldn't really see myself working for any of the local travel agencies. And I'd always wanted to do my own thing. So I decided it was now or never.

S   What did your wife think?

P   She wasn't too keen initially. She didn't want me turning her home into a travel agency. But thankfully it wasn't long before we could open a small office.

S   And business is still booming. Some of your services are expanding very rapidly.

P   Yes, they are. Core services like car rental were popular right from the word go, although what's really taken off is our monthly journal Travel Direct. Subscriptions are increasing at ten to twenty per cent a month. We're also looking at ways of promoting our currency exchange service.

S   So things are obviously going very well for you. But what exactly makes Corporate Direct so unique?

P   Well, although there are two other independent travel offices here in the area, offering people the same unbiased advice, as far as I know, we're still the only company keeping a comprehensive database of clients' travel guidelines, things like which airlines they use ...

S   ... meaning you make arrangements in line with each company's policies ...

P   Yes, that's right. And like the other big names, we can also provide very competitive rates too.

S   And as I understand it, you've also been developing the consultancy arm of the company as well. What services do you currently offer?

P   Well, advising companies on their travel policies is a very popular service and one which looks set to develop even further. What really attracts companies, though, is our corporate hospitality consultancy. We advise people on all sorts of PR type things, everything from winetasting to car-racing. We've also seen an increase in the number of clients asking our advice on language training courses.

S   But why does a company use an agency rather than make its own arrangements? Wouldn't it be cheaper?

P   Well, some companies do of course arrange things themselves. And in some cases it may indeed be cheaper for them to do so. But what's most important for companies, though, is that by using a corporate travel agency, they get everything arranged far more quickly, without the hassle of dealing with numerous providers. And I suppose our clients appreciate not having to worry about quality. Quite simply, we take the stress out of organising corporate travel.

S   So, who are your biggest clients?

P   Well, there's quite a range. We've got clients in the retail industry, like fashion companies, for example, and we're seeing far more interest from hotels and catering companies. Although, in general, I'd say our customers are more often than not from accountancy firms or banks and I can't see that changing in the future.

S   Speaking of the future, what new ventures are planned for Corporate Direct?

P   Well, we're introducing a 24-hour emergency service in the next two to three months. Clients will be able to call our Hotline for help at any time.

S   I should imagine that'll be really useful.

P   Well, we hope so. But our biggest priority at the moment is updating our Internet site in time for the Travel Fair in a fortnight's time. Clients will be able to access our website and book services directly from our home page. We're also considering introducing a Corporate Direct Credit Card, which will let clients settle their accounts with us on a monthly basis. But let's just say that's not exactly going to happen tomorrow.

S   Well, I'm afraid we'll have to finish there. Thank you Peter for talking to us today and congratulations again on your award.

**Exam focus: Speaking Test contains mock interviews.
No audioscript is provided.**

Unit 5a: Staff motivation

Listening (1.17–1.21)

Well, I've only been here a few months but I feel as if I've fitted in quite well so far. Everyone seems to have time to talk to me when I need help, which I really appreciate. The work's beginning to get interesting too. It's just that by now, I feel I really should be getting up to speed. Only it's a relatively new position and nobody's really spelt out what the exact scope of the job is or what my responsibilities and priorities should be. I think my line manager needs to give me a more concrete idea of what she expects me to achieve. She's back from holiday next week so maybe we could sit down together then.

Well, I get the feeling that we're starting to fall a bit behind other companies. I mean, when you look in the papers, you can't help noticing there's a bit of a gap between ourselves and the current going rate. I mean, it's not that I'm unhappy here or anything. I really like my job – it's interesting work and I think it's great that the job's so flexible. It's just that, at the end of the day, nobody likes to feel undervalued, do they? And in my position, it's not just myself I've got to think about. I've got responsibilities outside work as well.

Well, it's great to be part of a successful team. I don't think you could wish for harder-working or more dedicated colleagues. But I just sometimes think that our efforts aren't always rewarded. I know different managers have different styles but, well, everyone likes to feel appreciated, don't they? I mean, in my last job, managers always made a point of praising us when we beat our targets. One manager even used to encourage us to clap and cheer each other. And I must admit, I do miss that at times. I find praise here is sometimes a bit, shall we say, limited. It's like there's a 'That's what you're paid for' type of attitude.

I suppose, on the whole, I've got very little to complain about really. I get on with the rest of the team and that kind of thing. But there's one thing that's been on my mind for a while now. I just feel that, well, I've reached a stage where I'm capable of dealing with a lot more responsibility than I do at present. I just don't feel stretched any more. I don't feel as though I'm contributing as much as I could. It's almost as if I'm on autopilot. Things are beginning to feel a bit stale. What I need is a bit of variety, something to get my teeth into – a challenge.

Well, you're probably already aware of the fact that things aren't functioning too smoothly in Production at the moment. I don't know what other people have said but personally I think it's down to our procedures. There's no formal system for putting our ideas forward and in the past suggestions have just been ignored. I think management has to accept a lot of the responsibility. What we need to do is schedule regular meetings, which will improve the flow of information in both directions. I mean, at the moment I get more information through the shop floor grapevine than from my line manager.

Unit 5b: Recruitment

Listening (1.22)

Good afternoon. My name's Dave Archer and I'm here to tell you a little bit today about how the executive search process works. Now in Europe the executive search industry is worth $10bn a year, with a lot of that business being conducted in the UK. UK recruiters basically use one of four methods: there's **agency recruitment**, advertising selection (which is advertising in newspapers), a combination of selection and search and, at the top-end, executive search, otherwise known as headhunting. The executive search market is particularly prevalent in areas where market growth has been driven by **skills shortages** in client companies who are in a constant process of change. This is particularly the case in the finance, consulting and IT sectors, for example.

There's a fairly standard operating procedure for the delivery of headhunting assignments. It begins with a client giving a headhunter exclusive instruction and a brief to fill a vacancy. The headhunter's first task is to target potential companies, then individuals within those companies, either through **desk research** or through extensive contact networks. The headhunter then speaks to those individuals who match the specified criteria closely and are most appropriate for the job in question.

The headhunter then meets a number of potential candidates, either at their own offices or at a **neutral location**. Of course, these meetings have to be arranged and held with the utmost discretion. The headhunter then puts together the curriculum vitaes and **presents his findings** to the client. At this meeting the client is given a shortlist of about eight candidates and selects three or four of them for interview. This number gives a good chance of a successful candidate being hired. The candidates then go through the client's own interview procedure, possibly along with other candidates that applied directly to the company in response to an advertisement. Afterwards, the headhunter gives professional advice to both sides and facilitates the **offer process** to make sure that the whole assignment ends with a successful hire.

As for remuneration, the headhunter will receive a proportion, usually about 30 per cent, of the **first annual salary** of the person appointed. When a search company has been given an exclusive instruction to fill a vacancy, payment is normally billed in three instalments: first of all **a retainer**, then a second instalment upon submission of the shortlist and finally, a completion fee when the appointee starts with the client.

Now the advantage of a good headhunter is that he can provide a clear understanding of the business environment, a client's activities, their **strengths and weaknesses** and those of their rivals. This kind of comprehensive information can only be obtained through painstaking detective work, a close relationship with the **key players** in the industry and an international presence.

Headhunting is considered by many to be a 'black art' at best, unethical at worst. Yet at its highest levels, search is time and cost-efficient and provides a client with **commercially sensitive** information which would be otherwise unavailable. It targets those people who are happy in their current position, **motivated** and able to consistently deliver top performance – in other words, just the people who can benefit the client's growth plans and who cannot be accessed in any other way.

Model answers to Ex ❸, page 91

5b One-minute talk: How to fill a key vacancy 1.23

In order to fill a key vacancy, a company will usually follow the same standard procedure.

It will begin by producing an accurate job description of what it would like the successful candidate to do. From this, it can then produce a profile of this ideal candidate, which is a list of skills, experience, attributes and so on.

Having produced this profile, the company must then decide on the best recruitment method to capture a candidate with this profile. This might be an internal advertisement or an external advertisement in a newspaper, on the Internet say, even an agency or perhaps a headhunter.

Having decided on the best recruitment method, the advertisements are then placed or the headhunter contacted and a list of candidates will be then drawn up to be put through the company's recruitment processes. This might be interviews, psychometric tests or even hand-writing analysis. This will then produce the ideal candidate for the company.

The company will then have to negotiate terms with this candidate and, hopefully, this will result in terms which are both affordable for the company and attractive enough to get the candidate they want.

5b One-minute talk: The importance of having a good CV 1.24

Well, in my opinion, you can never underestimate the importance of having a good CV.

In the majority of cases, your CV is the employer's first impression of you, your first chance to impress your potential employer, let's say. It is the essential illustration of your suitability for the job, showing how your skills and experience match your employer's requirements

But more than that, it shows your ability to summarise, prioritise and present information effectively, essential skills in today's job market. It also shows your linguistic and communicative abilities.

Even though employers these days use a variety of selection techniques, such as analysing your handwriting, a good CV is still the single most important part of any application.

Unit 6a: Corporate culture

Listening I 1.25

I = Interviewer   MD = Managing Director

I And now to IKEA. The Swedish furniture retailer has just reported turnover of fifty-six billion Swedish kroner from its 150 stores worldwide. Now, IKEA puts its success down to corporate culture. So with me today to explain the secret of IKEA's culture is the Managing Director of IKEA UK. Good morning.

MD Good morning.

I Now is every IKEA store really exactly the same?

MD Well, in terms of culture they're pretty well uniform. Although our culture will naturally bond with the local culture to some extent, our core values such as simplicity and cost-consciousness are valid in all cultures. So we don't need to adapt the way we operate to run our stores. And as for products, although we make some minor adaptations to suit local tastes, we produce exactly the same catalogue in all twenty-eight countries.

I And where do these values originate?

MD It all goes back to Sweden in the 50s and 60s. IKEA's founder, Ingvar Kamprad, started the company at a time of democratic and social change …

I Are IKEA's values those of its founder, then?

MD Well, they have evolved over the last fifty-seven years, of course, but I think our mission statement 'A better life for the majority of people' still very much reflects the spirit of those early years. And Ingvar regularly visits IKEA stores around the world and talks to co-workers, especially on the shop floor.

I How does IKEA cope with such diversity amongst its employees?

MD Well, funnily enough, I've been working for IKEA for fifteen years in Sweden, Italy, Canada, the USA and here in the UK and what's struck me most is how much we have in common. People may interpret certain concepts such as responsibility and freedom differently but our core values such as humbleness exist in every country.

I So, what are the advantages of such a strong corporate culture?

MD They're tremendous. For one, there's a real bond between our operations around the world. It's easy to transfer across borders because you know the values will be exactly the same. And from a marketing and positioning point of view it's very advantageous as well. But the real pay-off is that it makes IKEA unique. You can clone our products and our store concept but not our culture. It takes years to build and it has to be maintained daily.

I But how do you educate 127,000 workers?

MD We begin by making sure people understand the values. That's why the IKEA Way seminars are so vital. All managers attend them and then it's their responsibility to pass the message on. Corporate culture also figures in meetings …

I Do you use educational videos and brochures as well?

MD Videos and brochures are helpful tools but only if used in conjunction with 'walking the talk' and discussing values with management. We have various initiatives which regularly provide co-workers with the opportunity to participate and contribute to these discussions.

I So, does culture affect IKEA's recruitment process?

MD It has a major impact. Although it's important for us to get highly skilled people into the company, we're not interested if there's a conflict of value systems. Anyone expecting a flash car or status symbols has no future with us. Recruitment at IKEA's an extensive process, based on judgements about a candidate's value systems and attributes. We can add retail skills, no problem, but it's tough to change someone's mindset.

I   Does that go for career advancement too?

MD Yes, it does.

I   So Swedish managers will always have more chance of promotion then?

MD We find that many Scandinavians identify more easily with our culture but there is no written or unwritten rule concerning the nationality of senior managers. It would be impossible, however, for anyone to advance within IKEA without wholly understanding and buying into the company's philosophy and culture. So every year senior managers are invited to an annual business meeting in Sweden where they are updated on plans and presented with the new range of products.

I   And finally, Ingvar Kamprad stepped down as President in the mid-80s, replaced by Anders Moberg. What effect did this have on the development of IKEA's culture?

MD Both Moberg and Chief Executive, Anders Dahlvig, have worked closely with Kamprad for many years and have a deep knowledge and understanding of Kamprad's original vision and philosophy. Naturally, IKEA is different today than it was primarily because it is three times bigger and has entered many more diverse and challenging markets. But our values and mission – to provide quality, affordable products for the majority of people – remain very much in situ.

Listening 2   1.26–1.30

Speaker 1

We organise anti-bureaucrat weeks, where all the managers have to work in the store showrooms, warehouses or restaurants for at least one week a year. The managers also have to work very hard at IKEA. In fact, the pace is such that we sometimes joke about 'management by running around'.

Speaker 2

The company's very informal. We dress casually and believe in a relaxed, open-plan office atmosphere. In countries like Germany and France, for example, we use informal terms of address such as 'du' and 'tu' rather than 'sie' and 'vous'. But this kind of environment actually puts pressure on management to perform because there's no security available behind status or closed doors.

Speaker 3

Ingvar constantly bypassed formal structures to talk directly with front-line managers. And whenever he visited a store, he tried to meet and shake hands with every employee, offering a few words of praise, encouragement or advice as he did so.

Speaker 4

Our entire east European strategy was mapped out by Ingvar on a small paper napkin. Just about every aspect of the entry strategy was laid out on this small piece of paper – we call it his Picasso. And for the past few years we've just built on and expanded that original version.

Speaker 5

There's also the story about Ingvar driving around town late one night checking out hotel prices till he found one economical enough. I've no idea whether it's true or not but I guess it's all part of the aura and the legend surrounding the man.

Unit 7a: Industrial espionage

Listening 1 1.31

J = Jill   O = Oliver   R = Rick

J   Good morning. Sorry I'm a little late. How did the board meeting go yesterday?

O   I didn't know there was a board meeting planned for yesterday.

R   There wasn't. It was an emergency meeting.

O   Emergency? Sounds exciting. What's the problem?

R   That's what we're here to talk about this morning. Close the door, would you Jill?

J   Yes, of course.

R   Thanks. Right, as you may know, we've lost several major contracts this year to Centronics, our biggest rival. Each time they've targeted the customer just as their contracts were up for renewal.

J   Are you saying they've somehow got access to our files?

R   Well, one of our customers was still loyal enough to inform us that Centronics seemed to have good information about the terms and conditions of their contract with us.

O   But surely, you don't think that someone's passing on that kind of information?

R   We don't know. That's the problem. And that's what we've got to find out. If there genuinely is a problem, then we'**ll have** to find out whether Centronics has infiltrated us or whether it's an inside job. So, we need to look at our systems and our people – and that's why you're both here.

Listening 2 1.32

O   So, what did you have in mind, Rick?

R   Well, first of all, Oliver, could someone have hacked into our intranet from outside?

O   Hack into the intranet? I doubt it. We've got pretty up-to-date security on the system.

J   Which means it's probably an inside job, right? Any ideas who it might be?

R   **If** I **knew that**, we **wouldn't be** here. So, we'll need to check out everyone who's joined us in the last twelve months.

J   The last twelve months? You don't think Centronics has placed a spy here, do you?

R   I'm not sure what to think, Jill. But we should check out their CVs anyway.

J   But it'**ll** take ages **if** we **do** that. Besides, their references would have been checked at the time anyway.

R   I know, but what about their previous employers? Were they checked?

J   Well ... we ... we don't normally ...

R   Exactly. I think it'**d** also **be** a good idea **if** you **looked** back at your appraisal records. See if you can find anyone who's disgruntled or making noises about wanting more money ...

J   Do you mean for the whole company or just Sales?

R   Well, start with Sales and then **keep** looking **if** you **don't find** anything. We've got to be thorough on this one. The board's taking it very seriously. Oliver, on the systems side of things, what can we do?

O   Well, I guess the first thing is to look at access. You know, see who's got access to what information.

R   Could you report back to me on that as soon as possible?

O   Sure. And I suppose I could also issue individual passwords so ...

R   That's true. And then we'**d know** exactly who was logging on, wouldn't we?

O   And what they were looking at – and when they were logging on.

J   How about email? Can we check people's email?

O   No problem, it's all automatically archived on the server. I'll get printouts for you, Rick.

J   And **if** I **could see** them, too, I **could see** who's dissatisfied and **have** a look at their appraisal notes and their personal record file.

O   OK.

J   That way I should be able to get an idea as to whether anyone's bearing a grudge.

O   Good idea, Jill. OK, do that. But make sure you do it discreetly. **If** word **got** out about this, then whoever's doing it **would stop** and **destroy** the evidence.

J   That's true. It **wouldn't do** much for morale either.

O   Which is already low enough around here at the moment.

R   Yes, this isn't exactly what we needed right now, is it?

J   What if we **don't come** up with anything, what **are** we **going** to do then?

R   The board's thinking about bringing in a security consultant. She'**d pose** as a temp in the Sales Department – you know, talk to people and get the gossip, find out who's unhappy and that kind of thing.

J   But I don't see the point. How **would** she **be able to** find out anything that we couldn't?

O   And it'**d** certainly **go** down well in Sales **if** they found out about it.

R   Yes, well ... Let's just hope it doesn't come to that.

Unit 7b: Business ethics

Listening 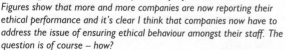 1.33–1.37

*I suppose, in a way, it's a kind of generation thing. When George started, there was no such thing as political correctness in the office environment. In those days, I'm sure it was common practice to call colleagues 'love' or 'darling', pay compliments about their figures or even give them gifts and things. But you just can't do that nowadays and he should have known better. He says his secretary never complained about it to him in person and that **if** she **had**, he**'d have stopped** doing it, but she didn't. Instead, she went straight to the board and warned them that she**'d take** legal action **if** nothing **was done** about it. Well, they soon hauled George in and explained the situation. George was outraged and told them what they could do with the job there and then.*

***If** you**'d looked** around the workplace, I guess you **would have seen** the evidence. I mean, in a company of this size you **would have expected** to see at least some ethnic diversity in the workplace, wouldn't you? Anyway, someone finally discovered a secret file with all the applicants who were not given an interview. Whoever it was blew the whistle to the local press and that was it – the company was faced with a PR disaster and a police investigation. Of course, the first thing the board did was give the well-paid HR executive his marching orders and insist that it was his prejudice and not company policy. But **if** that **was** the case, then why **hadn't** they **noticed** what was going on?*

*I'm sure Sharleen didn't think she was doing anything wrong at the time. She'd been told to put together a report on the market penetration of a new safety product we'd just launched. So she had to find out how much business our main rival was doing. OK, so hacking into their corporate intranet wasn't the right way of going about it – but no-one realised she was a complete whizzkid. Luckily, they didn't find out what happened. **If** they **had**, it **would have cost** us a fortune. You can imagine everyone's reaction when she announced what she'd done. Our Ethics Officer went mad and had to quickly put together an official code for dealing with competitors. As for Sharleen, well, she just got away without even so much as an official warning!*

*We'd been doing business with them for years and our sales executives had always enjoyed very good relationships with them. I don't think for one minute it **would have made** any difference **if** we **hadn't offered** them the occasional thank you for their business. But we always thought of it as good customer relationship management. What's wrong with the odd weekend away for a loyal customer? Anyway, the new CEO changed all that. Maybe it was a cultural thing, I don't know, but she suspended all freebies pending a review. She also recruited someone to regulate dealings with our clients – a sort of moral policeman, I guess. She even wrote to all our customers warning them not to accept any kind of presents from any of our reps.*

*Every business wants to be ethically sound but it's a hyper-competitive world out there and when you're under pressure to make money and keep to a budget, it's a different matter. Pete, the Production Manager, didn't like the new regulation spray paint – it just wasn't as good – so he carried on using the old stuff. He knew there**'d be** trouble **if** anyone **found out**. But I guess he just hoped they wouldn't. Of course, some campaigners tested the local water and found evidence of the banned chemicals. I suppose when you think about the PR nightmare that followed and the hefty fine the company had to pay, Pete was lucky to get away with just a letter threatening dismissal **if** he **used** the old paint ever again.*

Model answers to Ex ④, page 117

7b One-minute talk: How to encourage ethical behaviour from employees 1.38

Figures show that more and more companies are now reporting their ethical performance and it's clear I think that companies now have to address the issue of ensuring ethical behaviour amongst their staff. The question is of course – how?

To begin with, awareness is key. The company needs to set out an official code of ethical practice and ensure that all employees have access to it and can understand it easily. The company then needs to implement an effective and anonymous system of reporting any breaches of this code.

Once these procedures are in place, the company can then benchmark its ethical practice against those of industry leaders and see how it's doing. I think it's also vital that companies ensure that their senior managers set a good example, 'walk the talk' so to speak. If they don't behave ethically why should staff?

And finally, the company needs to put ethics high on the training and staff development agenda. It needs to make staff understand why ethics is important not just to the company but also to them as well.

7b One-minute talk: The importance of ethics in today's business world 1.39

Well, today globalisation is allowing companies to source from ever greater distances. This enables a company to exploit the economic advantages of low labour costs in one country and high market value in another.

Of course, they have to be careful not to be seen to be exploiting the workers. Consumers are becoming ever more sensitive to the exploitation stories and indeed environmental issues. This is because as consumers become richer and become used to spending more on a product, they also feel that they should be spending ethically. This is backed up by media stories and press items, and exploitation stories receive very good press. And of course, they can cause great damage. The bigger the brand, the higher the risk of a PR disaster.

Also companies are now having to worry about PR among their own employees. After all, recent stories about fat cat executive salaries can easily affect morale and thus workers' productivity.

Unit 8a: Global brands

Model answers to Ex ❸, page 125

8a One-minute talk: The importance of a global presence 1.40

With more mergers and acquisitions than ever before, I think it's becoming quite clear that a company in the future will need to have a global presence in order to compete in tomorrow's market place. This presence can give a company many competitive advantages.

To begin with, say, it can give access to local market knowledge, which can avoid some very, very expensive mistakes on account of cultural conflicts. Once more, it can spread the risk of doing business. If a company sells to more than one market, it can survive a downturn in any one of those markets, that's quite clear. And if a company becomes truly global, it can move its production around from country to country and take advantage of the best conditions at any given time. And the size of the company means it can realise economies of scale in advertising or distribution or shipping, for example.

So I think, all in all, when these things are taken into consideration, it's quite clear that any company not looking to establish a global presence in future may not have a future.

8a One-minute talk: How to promote an imported brand

With so many people these days making a conscious decision to buy domestic products, the pressure on those companies wishing to promote imported brands is greater than ever before.

Initially, a company needs to show how their product is superior to the local equivalents. Maybe it's better quality; maybe it's more stylish. A company needs to show customers the benefits of being more adventurous in their buying decisions to encourage them to move away from the current products they use. If you market a product as something exotic or unusual, you're bound to attract new clients. Cultural stereotypes are also a powerful selling tool. A cosmetics range associated with French chic, for example, is bound to attract customers. And if people are looking to buy a reliable car, there's no better label than 'made in Germany'. These national associations can also be exploited at the point of sale. Playing French music in supermarkets, for example, is proven to improve the sales of French wine.

Basically, if you want to successfully promote an imported brand, you need to give your customers a good reason to try something a little bit more exciting than their own home brands.

*Well, stereotypes are useful to advertisers because they're basically a
shorthand. You've got thirty seconds to get your main selling point across.
And with a stereotype you can establish a theme in two.*

*A stereotype is consistent and easily identifiable to a whole national group.
When a German audience see a Scotsman in a kilt, they instantly know
that the ad is going to be about economy. And they can make us feel
good about our own value systems or customs. We might pit a refined
Englishman against a brash New Yorker and that'll give the impression that
the product we're selling is obviously full of taste and discretion. And of
course, in this way, stereotypes are often identified with positive qualities.
For example, the German Audi designers in white lab coats are obviously
obsessed with perfection. And so we can guarantee that any product we buy
from them is going to be designed to perfection.*

*And lastly, stereotypes make good comedy because everybody wants
to laugh at other countries and people who are different. And of course, if
they've had a laugh, they're more likely to remember the advert.*

Unit 8b: Global sourcing

Listening 1.43

I = Interviewer   C = Craig

I   We keep hearing all about the globalisation of markets and supply chains
    and so on but why has global sourcing suddenly become so widespread?

C   Well, I think there are several factors, really. I mean, as companies expand
    internationally their outlook becomes increasingly global. What's more,
    hyper-competitive domestic markets have driven companies to look further
    afield in their search for competitive advantage. Although I think the process
    has really been accelerated by rapid advances in IT and telecoms. That's
    been the real catalyst for change.

I   And what's the great attraction? Why are companies so keen to
    source abroad?

C   It depends on the circumstances of the company in question. It could
    be anything from better access to overseas markets, lower taxes,
    lower labour costs, quicker delivery or a combination of any of these.

I   But it would be fair to say the financial benefits are the main
    incentive, wouldn't it?

C   In most cases it probably would, yes. Without them, I suppose few
    companies would be that interested. But there are risks involved as
    well, you know.

I   And what are those risks?

C   Well, the most common mistake companies make is they only see the
    savings and don't bother to think about the effect on other key criteria
    like quality and delivery. A clothing company that only buys from Asian
    suppliers at low cost, for instance, will find that as labour rates increase
    over time, it'll have to island hop to find new low cost sites. And this, of
    course, introduces uncertainty about quality – and that's critical for a
    clothing company. There are other possible risks as well.

I   Such as?

C   Well, such as negative publicity as a result of poor working
    conditions in the supplier's country. And, of course, there's always
    currency exchange risk.

I   So how do you go about weighing up all these factors and choosing a
    supplier?

C   It's crucial that companies know precisely what they're after
    from a supplier and that they fully understand their key selection
    criteria. They need to be careful to define them and make sure
    they're measurable and then rank them. It's dangerous selecting a
    particular supplier just because they happen to deliver outstanding
    performance in one objective such as cost or flexibility.

I   So, having selected a prospective partner, what then?

C   Well, then you have to negotiate how closely the two parties need
    to work together. If it's going to be a long-term relationship, you
    need to discuss how much sharing of information and resources will
    be necessary to extract maximum value from the collaboration. The
    prospective partners need to sit down and decide on the best form for
    the relationship to take.

I   And what's the most common form of this relationship?

C   Well, once again it depends on individual circumstances. The
    relationship can be anything, I suppose, from complete ownership
    through strategic alliances to buying the market.

I   Buying the market? What's that?

C   That's when companies just publish their specifications and ask
    prequalified vendors to bid for the contract. General Electric is
    currently doing $1bn of business this way over the Internet. It's a
    short-term deal with almost no interaction with the supplier and the
    length of the bidding process is cut by half. But most importantly for
    companies like GE, order processing is $5 an order as opposed to
    $50 when it's done on paper.

I   You mentioned strategic alliances. When do they make sense?

C   Well, for an aircraft manufacturer like Boeing, for example, an
    alliance with its engine manufacturers is logical because of the
    complex interaction between the body of the aircraft and its
    engines. And this complexity means everything has to be developed
    together. The arrangement also has the added bonus of reducing the
    financial risk of long-term development programmes.

I   And how about actually owning the supplier, then? When is that preferable?

C   Well, companies take over suppliers when they're vulnerable to
    fluctuations in the availability of key supplies. Take Du Pont, for
    example, the chemicals giant. Since oil is a primary ingredient
    of many of its products, Du Pont is very much affected by the
    availability, and therefore cost, of oil. Du Pont reduced these
    uncertainties by purchasing Conoco, its main oil supplier.

I   Thus keeping its costs down.

C   Possibly. Owning the supplier definitely increases financial control
    of the supply chain. But when you take the cost of acquisition into
    account, there are no short-term savings.

I   So, all in all, does global sourcing make sense?

C   Well, there are lots of very powerful benefits but managers have to
    consider all the main operational factors very carefully first.

Unit 8: Exam practice (Exam focus CD)

Listening Part One 2.08

*Good morning. First of all, thank you for inviting me to talk about our
electronic meetings system. I've got a handout to give you at the end. But
please feel free to make notes.*

*So, what is DecisionMaker®? Well, quite simply, it enables you to conduct
meetings either face-to-face or remotely using **networked computers**.
Now, you're probably wondering 'What's the point of using computers?'.
Well, the point is that unlike traditional meetings, everyone gets the
chance to contribute because they communicate through the keyboard.
This means people can communicate openly with no **fear of criticism**.
And believe me, that can make a big, big difference.*

*So what are the key advantages of DecisionMaker®? Well, first of all,
there is simultaneous input, meaning that everyone 'talks' at once –
although electronically, of course. This produces lots of contributions
as the process draws on the **creative energy** of the whole team – not
just individuals. Also, because ideas are submitted anonymously, people
are free to 'think the unthinkable'. Now this may not sound like much,
but believe me, it's a fantastic way of promoting **innovation** within your
company. It also means that all ideas are the property of the team –
which is a great boost to team spirit. And each suggestion is evaluated
on merit and not on feelings towards the person who came up with it.
Imagine that. A meeting without any personal politics.*

*With DecisionMaker®, ideas belong to the group. This means they are
analysed objectively without personal feelings interfering with the way
they are developed or rejected. Thus ideas are processed far more quickly
than in traditional meetings. And with everyone getting involved at the
same level, there is **no domination** of the proceedings by one or two
strong characters. What's more, because the meeting's conducted on
computers, everything is automatically recorded so there's no need for a
secretary to take notes or minutes. But of course, the real beauty of the
system is that you don't need to be in the same place – or even the same
country – to hold the meeting!*

So, how does it work? Well, let's look at some of the key features of DecisionMaker®. First of all, there's the Whiteboard®, which makes **drawings** produced during the meeting available to everyone else in the group. Pen passing and free-for-all drawings are also supported. Next we have FileShare®. With this function, the **distribution of documents** among the team couldn't be easier. Whether it's a spreadsheet, report or graphic image, just drag it into the FileShare window and it's accessible to the team. Thirdly, Consensus® gives instant feedback on suggestions by using one of three **voting methods**. There's the 10 Point Scale, Yes / No, and Agree/ Disagree. Once more, all votes are anonymous so honesty is guaranteed. And finally, there's Briefcase®, which lets you access your **favourite applications** during the meeting. If you want to use things like your calculator, your calendar or notepad, simply drag them into the Briefcase and they'll be available whenever you need them.

Right, I'd now like to demonstrate just how the system works.

Part Two 2.09

I'm quite well organised really so I have no problems dealing with things like credit notes and invoices. What I do find stressful, though, is having to deal with people when they ring up and complain about damaged goods or a late delivery. We're only a small company, you know, so it's up to me and my colleague to sort things out. Although, having said that, my colleague isn't actually that big a help at all. She spends most of her day gossiping to friends, so people can only get through to my extension. It's no good trying to interrupt her either. She just shrugs her shoulders and carries on. It's very irritating, you know.

My new colleague's really nice. She worked in Despatch up until about three months ago, so she's already familiar with all the forms and things we use here at the company. I've started her off on some basic procedures, like paying salaries and dealing with credit control, which means that I can concentrate on preparing for next month's audit. She's doing quite well actually – well, when she finally makes it into the office, that is. It's almost twenty past by the time she's gets in ... and even later if she goes to the canteen to get something to eat first. I think she just goes there for a good gossip with her friends from Despatch, myself.

Well, I sometimes struggle to keep my cool with the Sales Department always on at us to get things moving more quickly. We're busy enough as it is, what with planning and organising operations, scheduling projects and dealing with plant maintenance. It doesn't help having to share such a small space with my boss. Well, we get on all right even though he's quite a tidy person and I tend to leave the place in a bit of a mess. But what really does annoy me is the amount of time I have to spend unjamming the printer or the photocopier after he's been using it. I just find it so inconsiderate of him to leave me to deal with it all the time.

I'm used to keeping records of prices and ordering office supplies, of course, but I never realised there would be so much to the job. I mean, when I think back to the interview, the Personnel Manager didn't mention half the things I'm now doing. I've never had to actually select the suppliers myself before. It's a real balancing act, getting the right product at the right price. But my colleague's given me lots of useful information. In fact, there isn't much he hasn't told me. We took a break together on my first day here and he didn't waste any time telling me all about everyone in the office. It makes me wonder now what he's saying behind my back.

It's been a real nightmare lately. We're busy enough at the best of times. And now we've lost our admin assistant, it's even worse. I've been up to my neck in paperwork, going through contract details with the Legal Department and checking CVs and references. You know, I've interviewed forty applicants this week already for one of our vacancies and it's only Wednesday today. My colleague seems to take everything in his stride, though. If he's not standing next to the fax machine chatting to someone from the Purchasing Department, he's outside my window smoking. Look, there he is, lighting up again. I can't believe it. That's his sixth one this morning. Honestly, it's a wonder he gets any work done at all.

Part Three 2.10

J = Jim   S = Sally

J   Welcome to Working Hours. In studio today we have Sally Michaels, HR Director at ZSV Insurance, one of many companies promoting flexible working schemes. Hello, Sally.

S   Hello, Jim.

J   So, Sally, what made ZSV decide to move away from the rigid nine to five?

S   Well, social changes have been a major factor. More women are now returning to work after having children, for example. And, even more importantly, we've had to cater for changing customer demands. With customers now preferring to do their business over the phone, we need our staff to work more flexible hours. We also took over two smaller companies recently. So we wanted a common scheme to unite all our new employees.

J   So what are the advantages of the scheme for ZSV?

S   Well, for one thing, we put great emphasis on providing our staff with regular, high quality training. It costs a lot of time and money to train our employees. So, obviously, it makes sense to retain them.

J   And providing them with flexible working patterns can help you do that?

S   That's right. But that isn't the main benefit. We see the scheme as primarily a tool for attracting potential staff to our company – especially high-calibre graduates.

J   Speaking of your staff, what's the main attraction for them?

S   Well, the majority of people in the scheme want to spend more time improving their qualifications by doing an MBA or something like that.

J   I imagine the scheme must make it much easier for staff to look after their children too.

S   Yes, that is an added benefit, as is being able to dedicate more time to their outside interests, such as sports.

J   Now, I believe the scheme isn't totally new.

S   That's right. There was an old scheme but awareness of it was very low. Most men, for example, assumed it was only available to women, which, of course, wasn't the case. The new scheme will also continue to offer alternative working patterns to staff on both short and longterm contracts. Only this time, we're making it available to employees at all levels of the organisation and not just people in more junior positions.

J   I see. And what do you think will be the most popular element of the scheme? Flexible hours?

S   It's difficult to say at the moment but, yes, flexitime is likely to be popular. Typically, though, with the old scheme, employees showed most interest in having longer breaks from work, and I expect it'll be the same this time. There might be some interest in, say, job share arrangements in the future. But we'll have to wait and see.

J   And ZSV is also encouraging teleworking, I believe.

S   Yes, we are.

J   Now, how does that work? Do you use video-conferencing, for example?

S   Well, we have the facilities but they're not that widely used at the moment. As most of our teleworkers have access to the company network, they tend to communicate electronically. It's far more convenient than telephoning because you don't have to worry about whether the person's available or not.

J   That's interesting. But what about your managers, what challenges do they face working from home?

S   Well, several have mentioned the need to be self-disciplined, differentiating between work-time and private time. But the biggest difficulty seems to be empowering others to act for you, especially when they're in the office and you're not.

J   That's surprising. I would have thought the most difficult thing would be staying motivated without the support of colleagues.

S   Well, that's not something that's come up so far but I'm sure it will.

J   So, how do employees get selected as teleworkers?

S   Well, it all begins with an interview with your line manager.

J   To discuss whether the home environment is suitable, you mean?

S   Well, it's not quite as simple as that. The main reason we have the interview is to ascertain whether the applicant's duties are compatible with working from home. It's easier, say, for an IT specialist to work from home than a PA. If the interview goes OK, we then introduce the applicant to a colleague with personal experience of teleworking. We think it's important for the applicant to hear what it's really like working on your own at home.

J   Well, I'm afraid time's running out so we'll have to stop there. Thank you, Sally, for joining us today.

Answer key

Unit 1a: Work roles (Self-study)

Ex ❶:

1	A	2	C	3	C	4	C
5	A	6	B	7	A	8	C

Ex ❷: *Suggested answer:*

1 The company has just set up a new job share system.

2 He was given feedback on his performance during his job appraisal.

3 Her job description didn't outline her main duties and responsibilities very clearly.

4 I'm really enjoying my new job.

5 The employees carried out the job as soon as they were given their brief.

6 WorkSet was used to classify and highlight aspects of the job.

7 One of the most important things in this job is the ability to communicate.

8 We need to monitor the way he carries out his job.

Ex ❸:

2 It was suggested that some training should be/be organised for our team leaders.

3 It was decided that a consultant should be brought in/be brought in/to bring in a consultant.

4 It was found that team leaders' roles are not/were not clear enough.

5 It was agreed that we should start/we start implementing WorkSet the following month.

6 We recommend that Ekstrom should set up/ sets up/set up new assessment centres.

Ex ❹:

2 hold
3 says
4 aren't/are not delegating
5 doesn't/does not seem to be getting
6 's/is even bringing
7 think
8 I'm/I am definitely getting

Unit 1b: Company structure (Self-study)

Ex ❶:

2	virtual team	3	corporate intranet
4	line manager	5	business environment
6	hierarchical organization	7	on-line support
8	operating costs		

Ex ❷:

Verb	Noun	Adjective
standardize	**standardization**	**standard/ standardised**
diversify	diversity	**diverse/ diversified**
respond	**response/ responsiveness**	responsive

operate	operation	**operating**
suit	**suitability**	suitable
supervise	supervision	**supervisory**
vary	**variety**	varied

Ex ❸:

1	remote	2	sequential	3	virtual
4	specify	5	back up	6	interaction
7	challenge	8	impact	9	e-mail
10	motivation				

Ex ❹:

1	into	2	for	3	under
4	on	5	with	6	on

Ex ❺:

1	Correct	2	those	3	such
4	Correct	5	have	6	Correct
7	lot	8	Correct	9	themselves
10	Correct	11	and	12	the
13	Correct				

Ex ❻:

2 've/have just promoted

3 hasn't/has not even been working **or** hasn't/has not even worked

4 did she join

5 told

6 saw

7 's/has broken

8 's/has been looking

9 thought

10 was

11 's/has made

12 have already been calling

13 's/has he taken **or** did he take

14 didn't/did not mention

Unit 1: Exam practice

R1:

1	D	2	C	3	B	4	E
5	A	6	B	7	E	8	C

R5:

1	well	2	their
3	from	4	on
5	a	6	the
7	is	8	more
9	up	10	such

Unit 2a: Stocks and shares (Self-study)

Ex ❶:

1	peak	2	level off
3	general upward trend	4	fluctuate
5	bottom out	6	recover

Ex ❷:

1	shares	2	flotation
3	broker	4	investment
5	listings	6	commission
7	merger	8	dividends

Ex ❸:

1	Neutral	2	Positive
3	Negative	4	Positive
5	Negative	6	Negative
7	Positive	8	Neutral

Ex ④: **Suggested answer:** *(108 words)*

This year, April sales of Fresh 'n' Cool reached 725,000 units, which was slightly down on last year. May saw sales fall to 700,000 units before they began to make a recovery, rising steadily to peak at 1.3m units in July. In August, they fell slightly, to 1.25m units.

In contrast to this year's poor performance in spring, last year's sales rose between April and July, from 750,000 to over 1.25m units. However, they then fell sharply in August, finishing back at their April level of 750,000 units.

Therefore, although sales of Fresh 'n' Cool were initially down on last year, they finished much more strongly this year.

Ex ⑤: *At the start of 2006, shares in Octavian Cotton stood at $160. However, by the end of the year they **had collapsed** to just $50. They recovered **steadily** over the next twelve months but **fluctuated** sharply all through 2008. In 2009 they continued their **recovery**, **climbing** to $160 per share, where they remained throughout 2010.*

*Shares in Minchin Textiles starting trading at $150. Like Octavian, Minchin saw its shares fall during 2006 and then **pick up** the following year. This recovery then **turned** into a general upward trend, **which** continued until late 2009, when shares peaked at $220. They then collapsed before **rising** briefly to just over $150 at the end of 2010.*

Unit 2b: Mergers and acquisitions (Self-study)

Ex ❶:

Acquired another company	Merged with another company	Was acquired by another company
Lloyds TSB	BP	HBOS
RBS	Glaxo Welcome	ABN Amro
HSBC	SmithKline Beecham	Household International
Vodafone		National Westminster Bank
		Mannesmann

Noun + noun or adj + noun	Prefix + noun
long-term	sub-prime
hat-trick	mega-mergers
fee-paying	re-establishing
Empire-building	
deal-makers	
self-interest	

Ex ❷:

1	takeover	2	merging
3	growth	4	competitive
5	benefits	6	streamline
7	restructuring	8	acquisition

Ex ❸:

2 integrate different cultures
3 add long-term value
4 undercut competitors' prices
5 reduce operating costs
6 generate cost improvements

Ex ❹:

1	to	2	represents/is	3	that
4	its	5	whether	6	not
7	while	8	such		

Ex ❺:

*The merger raises a number of HR issues (1) **which/that** will need to be addressed as a matter of urgency and in a manner (2) **which/that** is seen to be fair to the employees of both companies. Firstly, the pay structures of the two companies, (3) **which** show marked differences, will need to be reviewed and harmonised. Furthermore, redundancy terms will have to be agreed and offered to employees (4) **who/that** lose their jobs as a result of the merger. This is particularly important with regard to senior managers (5) **whose** contracts contain severance clauses (6) **which/that** guarantee them generous terms. Our approach to these job cuts, (7) **which** were promised to shareholders as part of the terms of the merger, will also have a major effect on staff morale within the newly-formed company. It is imperative that we avoid any deterioration of staff morale, (8) **which** could have an adverse effect on company performance.*

*NB: If **which** or **who** can be replaced by **that**, no comma is used.*

Unit 2: Exam practice

R2:	1	D	2	C	3	E		
	4	F	5	G	6	A		

R4:	1	C	2	B	3	A	4	C
	5	D	6	C	7	A	8	D
	9	B	10	B				

R5:	1	had	2	what	3	as
	4	out	5	many	6	such
	7	no	8	all	9	which
	10	their				

R6A:	1	order	2	a	3	been
	4	Correct	5	which	6	Correct
	7	in	8	the	9	but
	10	Correct	11	be	12	you

R6B:	1 they	2 Correct	3 Correct
	4 have	5 Correct	6 that
	7 of	8 Correct	9 to
	10 a	11 make	12 for

Unit 3a: Trade fairs (Self-study)

Ex ❶:

1 a	2 Correct
3 Correct	4 Correct
5 which	6 Correct
7 it	8 these
9 Correct	10 and
11 Correct	12 are

Ex ❷:

```
1 a d v e r t i s e m e n t
          2 r e p l y
3 a p p l i c a t i o n
              4 d e s i g n
        5 e v e n t s
    6 b e n e f i t s
          7 s t a n d s
      8 r e t a i l e r s
9 b r o c h u r e s
```

Ex ❸:
2 With reference to your letter of
3 We look forward to meeting you
4 Further to our conversation of
5 Should you have any further questions
6 Please do not hesitate to contact me

Ex ❹:
2 lands
3 get
4 arrive
5 will take/is going to take/is taking
6 have checked in
7 get
8 go

Unit 3b: Entering a market (Self-study)

Ex ❶:
seminars
trip
association
practices
norms
card
acquaintance
negotiations

Ex ❷:

1 invest in	2 intend to
3 amount to	4 build on
5 allow for	6 participate in
7 respond to	8 enquire about

Ex ❸:

make	do	enter into
conversation	a mailshot	a joint venture
an investment	business	a partnership
a request	research	a relationship
a commitment	preparatory work	

Ex ❹: *Suggested answer:* (109 words)

Doing business in London and Beijing

Overall, it is far cheaper to do business in Beijing than in London, with the most dramatic differences in the areas of office space and salaries. Renting office space is ten times cheaper in Beijing than in London. Likewise, a bilingual secretary in Beijing earns barely a tenth of the going rate in London. The cost of a local phone call is also more reasonable, as is the average cost of accommodation at a five-star hotel.

The single area in which Beijing outstrips London in terms of cost is rent, with the price almost double that of a comparable property in London.

Ex ❺:
2 forge relationships
3 pledge investment
4 produce trade literature
5 swap business cards
6 provide hospitality
7 start proceedings
8 match needs

Ex ❻: At meetings with **the** Chinese, **the** leader of your group will be expected to enter first and will generally be offered **a** seat beside **the** most senior Chinese person present. This person will usually chair **the** meeting and act as **the/---** host. At **the** beginning of **the** meeting, all **the** people present will greet each other and swap business cards, after which **a** period of small talk begins. **The** host will then officially start **the/---** proceedings with **a** brief introduction to **the** Chinese enterprise. **The** visiting team is then invited to speak. It is appropriate at this point for foreign participants to make their case and answer questions. Following **the** meeting **the** Chinese enterprise will probably arrange **a** special dinner for **the** overseas guests along with other entertainment such as sightseeing. Guests should always accept these invitations as small talk in **a** social setting is essential for forging relationships with **the** Chinese.

Unit 3: Exam practice

R3:	1 B	2 C
	3 D	4 D
	5 B	6 A

W2: **Suggested answer:** (229 words)

Dear Mr Salter

Re: Reference for Mr John Bridge

Further to your letter dated 15 October, I am writing concerning the application of John Bridge for the position of Training Manager at STC International.

I have known John for over fifteen years, and feel that the length of our friendship, together with my personal experience of working as Training Manager at Tarbus UK, allows me to comment on his suitability for the advertised position.

As you are aware, John is currently employed by Tarbus UK as Training Co-ordinator for the busy Marmouth branch, where his main responsibility is to assess the training needs of the employees and arrange training programmes to meet these needs. This involves liaising with a large number of language and business skills organisations as well as evaluating the effectiveness of the training employees receive.

John has excellent interpersonal skills and is sociable, patient and a good listener. As a friend, I particularly appreciate his loyalty and sense of humour. I also admire the calm and logical way in which he approaches difficult situations.

I have no hesitation in recommending him for the position of Training Manager for your company and wish him every success in his application.

If you have any further questions, please do not hesitate to contact me, either at the above address or on (01420) 655567.

Yours sincerely

Julia Shipton
Training Manager

Unit 4a: The future of work (Self-study)

Ex ❶:
| 1 | Negative | 2 | Positive | 3 | Negative |
| 4 | Negative | 5 | Positive | 6 | Positive |

Ex ❷:
1	C	2	A	3	B
4	A	5	B	6	A
7	B	8	C		

Ex ❸:
2 foster team spirit
3 key a number into a telephone terminal
4 run out of supplies
5 show interest
6 centralise operations
7 adapt to a new way of working
8 vacate premises

Ex ❹:
| 1 | between | 2 | on | 3 | on |
| 4 | to | 5 | into | 6 | on |

Ex ❺: meet needs, spend time, run a meeting, predict needs, suit needs, hold a meeting, waste time

Ex ❻:
2 It is unlikely that the office will cease to be important.
3 The Internet looks set to explode.
4 More people are bound to want to work from home.
5 It is improbable that everyone will want have an iPad®.
6 Working from home will undoubtedly increase in future.

Unit 4b: e-business (Self-study)

Ex ❶:
1	no/little	2	their	3	that/how
4	but	5	such	6	the
7	any	8	which/that		

Ex ❷:

¹i	n	t	e	r	n	e	t	
	²w	e	b	s	i	t	e	
		³b	u	l	l	e	t	i	n	s
⁴t	r	a	n	s	a	c	t	i	o	n	s
	⁵o	n	l	i	n	e		
		⁶i	n	t	r	a	n	e	t
⁷i	n	t	e	g	r	a	t	e
⁸b	r	o	w	s	e	r		
	⁹c	u	s	t	o	m	e	r	s

Ex ❸:
2 manage inventories
3 improve operating efficiencies
4 handle transactions
5 communicate with partners
6 analyse customer behaviour
7 personalise offerings
8 anticipate customer wants

Ex ❹:
2 after-sales service
3 product support
4 staff turnover
5 customer base
6 distance learning

Ex ❺: **Suggested answer:**
2 We'll be doing more on-line training in future.
3 She won't have finished the report by the end of next week.
4 We won't be using any paper invoices next year.
5 He will have completed the website by July.
6 I'll be rethinking our internet strategy over the next few weeks.
7 Internet usage will have doubled within five years.
8 We won't be launching the products until the website has been completed.

Unit 4: Exam practice

L1:
1	1975	2	popularity	
3	suitable premises	4	rapid expansion	
5	substantial contracts	6	resources and knowledge	
7	high-street chemist	8	new factory	
9	brand name	10	marketing operations	
11	family atmosphere	12	market leader	

L2:
13	D	14	B	15	C	16	E
17	G	18	N	19	K	20	J
21	L	22	M				

L3:
23	A	24	C	25	B	26	B
27	C	28	A	29	A	30	A

R4:
1	B	2	C	3	D	4	A
5	C	6	A	7	D	8	A
9	B	10	C				

Unit 5a: Staff motivation (Self-study)

Ex ❶:
1	being	2	which
3	Correct	4	Correct
5	such	6	Correct
7	of	8	any
9	Correct	10	those
11	certain	12	Correct
13	the	14	Correct

Ex ❷:
1	ineffective	2	insignificant
3	unsatisfactory	4	irregular
5	unappreciated	6	inflexible
7	irresponsible	8	uninteresting
9	incapable	10	unspecific

1	unappreciated	2	incapable
3	interesting	4	specific
5	irregular	6	ineffective
7	inflexible	8	irresponsible

Ex ❸:
2	restore	repair
3	schedule	plan
4	appreciate	value
5	sever	cut
6	rename	rebrand
7	address	deal with
8	quit	resign

Ex ❹:
1	into	2	from	3	towards/to
4	behind	5	of	6	as

Ex ❺:
2	are awarded
3	are not based
4	has been criticised
5	was introduced
6	have been noticed
7	will be/is going to be reviewed
8	are currently being encouraged
9	is also provided/has also been provided
10	can be found

Unit 5b: Recruitment (Self-study)

Ex ❶:
1. The client instructs the headhunter to fill a vacancy.
2. The headhunter identifies possible candidates.
3. The candidates are interviewed by the headhunter.
4. The headhunter provides a shortlist of candidates.
5. Candidates go through the client's selection process.
6. The client appoints one of the candidates.
7. The client pays the headhunter his completion fee.

Ex ❷:
2. extension number
3. future reference
4. executive search
5. neutral location
6. key player
7. sensitive information
8. skills shortage

Ex ❸:
1	on	2	on	3	for
4	into	5	to	6	across
7	in	8	with	9	to

Ex ❹:
2. present findings
3. shortlist candidates
4. pay a retainer
5. conduct business
6. compile a list

Ex ❺: **Suggested answer:**

1. The recruitment agency claims there is an acute skills shortage in the IT sector.
2. For recruitment purposes we need an up-to-date copy of your CV.
3. Advertising a job vacancy in newspapers is one recruitment method; using an agency is another.
4. If you're looking for a job, why not apply to a recruitment agency?
5. When recruiting new staff, we look for evidence of exceptional past performance.
6. I have shortlisted candidates with the qualities which we know to be necessary from our previous experience of recruitment.
7. Before he was appointed, he had to go through the client's internal recruitment process.
8. Using a headhunter to recruit a new employee can save a company time.

Ex ❻:
Verb	Noun
apply	**application**
appoint	appointment
compare	**comparison**
explain	**explanation**
categorise	category
recruit	**recruitment**

Ex ❼: | 2 which | 3 its | 4 which
| 5 those | 6 which | 7 This
| 8 who/that | 9 this/such | 10 these/the

Unit 5: Exam practice

R1: | 1 B | 2 C | 3 E | 4 A
| 5 D | 6 C | 7 B | 8 E

R5: | 1 which | 2 unlike
| 3 however | 4 only
| 5 each | 6 a
| 7 such | 8 both/each
| 9 one | 10 than

Unit 6a: Corporate culture (Self-study)

Ex ❶: | 1 A | 2 A | 3 B | 4 C
| 5 C | 6 B | 7 A | 8 A

Ex ❷: | 1 adaptations | 2 competitors
| 3 operations | 4 promotional
| 5 interpretations | 6 expansion
| 7 influential | 8 perceptive

Ex ❸: | 2 similar | alike
| 3 informal | casual
| 4 fresh | new
| 5 economical | thrifty
| 6 vital | crucial
| 7 tough | hard
| 8 global | worldwide

Ex ❹: | 2 arriving | 3 operating
| 4 restructuring | 5 working
| 6 (to) increase | 7 realising
| 8 to be | 9 to let
| 10 believe | 11 confronting
| 12 to turn | 13 to reflect
| 14 looking | 15 modernising
| 16 to be

Unit 6b: Cultural diversity (Self-study)

Ex ❶: | 1 means that | 2 However
| 3 while | 4 therefore
| 5 as opposed to | 6 although/while
| 7 Similarly

Ex ❷: *Suggested answer:* (133 words)

Mustermann AG and Svensson AB
The graph shows the changing number of employees at Mustermann and Svensson from 2006 to 2010. Looking at the general trend, there has been an upward movement in the number of employees at Svensson whereas Mustermann has seen numbers fall dramatically over the same period.

During 2006 and 2007 there were 175,000 employees at Svensson. Employee numbers rose steadily over the following three years to reach 210,000 in 2010.

On the other hand, from 2006 to 2009 Mustermann saw employee numbers fall from 230,000 to an all-time low of below 175,000. In 2010, however, Mustermann felt sufficiently confident to start taking on new employees once more with the result that by the end of the year employee levels stood at 185,000, slightly higher than the figure for 2008.

Ex ❸: | 2 fix salary levels
| 3 conduct a meeting
| 4 appreciate differences
| 5 build understanding
| 6 solve a dilemma
| 7 follow a strategy
| 8 hold a belief

Ex ❹:

Verb	Noun
choose	**choice**
succeed	success
expect	**expectation**
affect	effect
pay	**pay/payment**
believe	**belief**
solve	solution
promote	**promotion**
diversify	diversity
examine	**examination**
preserve	preservation

Ex ❺: | 2 We needn't have gone there.
| 3 We shouldn't have adapted the product.
| 4 We ought to be getting back.
| 5 The language problems can't have helped.
| 6 They might be having trouble working together.

Unit 6: Exam practice

R3: | 1 A | 2 C | 3 C
| 4 D | 5 B | 6 B

W2A: *Suggested answer:* (226 words)

Report

Cost-cutting: Administration Department

Introduction
The aim of this report is to examine ways of cutting costs in the Administration Department and explain the implications of these cuts for the running of the department. It is based on the results of a detailed questionnaire sent to all employees.

Findings

It is clear that within the department there are a number of areas where cost-cutting measures could be taken. The most significant areas of concern are the following:

- paper
- refreshments.

Recommendations

In order to deal with the issue of paper, it is suggested that the department installs a system to recycle all used printing and photocopying paper. It is expected that by adopting new recycling procedures, the department could save as much as £100 a month.

As for refreshments, it is recommended that tea and coffee should only be offered free to employees during morning and afternoon breaks. At all other times employees should be required to pay for refreshments. This measure should reduce the company's monthly bill for refreshments from £320 to £110, thereby making a saving of over £200.

Conclusion

It is felt that the above measures will result in immediate and substantial savings for the Administration Department. Although these recommendations are not expected to affect the running of the department in any significant way, managers should be prepared to encounter initial resistance from staff.

R4:

1	D	2	C	3	C	4	A
5	A	6	B	7	B	8	A
9	B	10	D				

R5:

1	is	2	although/while	3	with
4	what	5	not	6	for
7	both/all	8	the	9	as
10	few				

W2B: **Suggested answer:** (247 words)

Dear Mr Schommartz

Re: Work placement at Shiptols UK, 1 Feb 2000 – 31 July 2000

Further to your appointment as Trainee Public Relations Assistant, I would like welcome you to Shiptols UK. I would also like to take this opportunity to provide you with some introductory information, both about the company itself and the duties you will be expected to perform during your time here. I trust you will find the following points useful.

Unlike many of our overseas subsidiaries, Shiptols UK is divided into seven main departments:

Production, Research and Development, Finance, Personnel, Sales, Marketing and Public Relations. I work in the Public Relations department, which is headed by Jenny Holloway. Public Relations is the smallest department in the company, consisting of fifteen employees, who usually work in teams of five. As my assistant, you will generally report directly to me.

My job mainly involves communicating with our local distributors. However, I am currently in charge of organising a major press launch for our new 'Easywash' washing powder, which is due to take place on 15 April. Initially you will be working with Claire O'Reilly, who is responsible for designing the information packs for the press launch. Your duties will include helping to write articles for the pack and choosing photographs for inclusion.

I look forward to working with you in the near future. In the meantime, if you have any further questions, please contact me on (+44) 1431 23776.

Yours sincerely

Martin Wallis
Communications Officer

Unit 7a: Industrial espionage (Self-study)

Ex ❶: ***Examples of industrial espionage:***
infiltrate a competitor, bug an office, hack into a network, leak sensitive information, steal confidential data, resort to shady practices

Measures against industrial espionage:
monitor photocopier use, shred important documents, bring in a security adviser, identify a perpetrator, protect a computer system, install passwords

Ex ❷:

1	this	2	Correct	3	of
4	been	5	to	6	Correct
7	Correct	8	who	9	Correct
10	by	11	it	12	a

Ex ❸:

Verb	Noun	Adjective
accept	**acceptance/acceptability**	acceptable
suspect	**suspect/suspicion**	**suspect/ suspicious**
imitate	imitation	**imitation**
access	**access/accessibility**	**accessible**
analyse	**analysis**	**analytical**
secure	security	**secure**
protect	**protection**	**protective**
copy	copy	**copiable**
identify	**identity/identification**	**identifiable**

confuse	**confusion**	**confused/**
		confusing
isolate	**isolation**	**isolated**
break	**breakage/breach**	broken
measure	**measure/measurement**	**measurable**

Ex ❹: 2 call the police   3 bear a grudge
4 devise a system   5 break the law
6 suspect foul play   7 shred paperwork
8 take measures

Ex ❺: **Suggested answer:**
3 're/are
4 can go
5 's/is
6 'd be/would be
7 could also look
8 can give
9 like
10 doesn't have/does not have
11 do you still want
12 didn't find/did not find
13 doesn't/does not need to
14 's/has
15 's found/has found
16 'll put

Unit 7b: Business ethics (Self-study)

Ex ❶: workplace safety, sexual harassment, racial discrimination, conflict of interest, environmental issues, product safety, competitive practices, privacy, executive salaries, gifts and entertainment/corporate gift-giving, corporate philanthropy, whistle-blowing, legal compliance, fair employment practices, delivery of high quality goods and services, industrial espionage, financial mismanagement

2 sexual harassment   3 workplace safety
4 legal compliance   5 executive salaries
6 corporate gift-giving   7 racial discrimination
8 whistle-blowing

Ex ❷: 1 illegal   2 unethical
3 unfair   4 unlawful
5 incorrect   6 unofficial

Ex ❸:
2	measure	precaution
3	conduct	behaviour
4	rule	regulation
5	threat	warning
6	rival	competitor
7	freebie	gift

Ex ❹:
1	who	2	to
3	more	4	did
5	when	6	on
7	that	8	as
9	else	10	a
11	when	12	'd/had

Ex ❺: **Suggested answer:**

2 The boss would have sacked him by now if he weren't the Managing Director's nephew.

3 If we hadn't got that contract, the company wouldn't have survived the recession last year.

4 I'm sure she would have been dismissed if anyone had found out how she was getting her information.

5 If she hadn't been filmed shredding the files, she'd still be working here today.

6 The problem would have been solved more quickly if the company had brought in a consultant earlier.

7 The company wouldn't have known if the new assistant hadn't blown the whistle to the press.

8 If he'd left sooner than he did, the company wouldn't be having all the bad publicity it is right now.

Unit 7: Exam practice

R2:
1	C	2	E	3	A
4	G	5	D	6	B

R6:
1	Correct	2	the	3	which
4	with	5	Correct	6	and
7	that	8	what	9	Correct
10	you	11	Correct	12	a

W2A: **Suggested answer:**   (245 words)

Dear Sir

I am writing to apply for the position of Personal Assistant advertised in this month's edition of 'PA Journal Today'. I feel that my experience of working as a PA and a secretary would prove valuable to your company and that I can offer the IT and language skills required for the post.

As you will see from my enclosed CV, I am currently employed by Garners Ltd, where I have been working as PA to the Sales Director, Mr Michael Smart, for the last three years. At Garners my duties include dealing with Mr Smart's correspondence, keeping his diary and organising all his business travel, both in the

UK and overseas. Previously, I was employed by Whitehead Ltd as Senior Secretary in the Sales Department, where, in addition to routine secretarial work, my responsibilities included organising internal sales meetings and dealing with clients visiting the company.

As well as developing my IT skills by taking courses in Excel and Powerpoint at a local college, I have also recently passed A-level French (Grade B) to add to the A-level in German I gained last year. I am particularly interested in the position of Personal Assistant at your company as it will enable me to use my IT and foreign language skills to the full.

I look forward to hearing from you in the near future. If you require any further information, please do not hesitate to contact me on (0181) 64572.

Yours faithfully

W2B: **Suggested answer:** (240 words)

Report

Working conditions

Introduction
The aim of this report is to assess the main reasons for staff complaints about working conditions and propose ways of improving the situation. It is based on the results of a detailed questionnaire sent to all employees in addition to in-depth interviews with managers and union representatives.

Findings
As might have been expected, low pay is the main reason for staff complaints. Furthermore, a significant number of employees are not satisfied with the current level of bonus payments and fringe benefits. Another major complaint is the employees' working environment. In particular, poor ventilation and lighting in communal areas such as the canteen and coffee room have been highlighted.

Recommendations
In order to deal with the issue of pay, it is recommended that a meeting should be arranged with union representatives to discuss both a review of pay levels and the launch of a range of incentive schemes. This could, for example, lead to the introduction of performance related top-ups, with bonuses being awarded to those employees who exceed a target level of performance per week. In addition, employees

who have been with the company for over two years could be entitled to a range of fringe benefits, such as subsidised private health care arrangements. It is also suggested that employees are offered an opportunity to express their views on improving their working environment by using a Suggestions Box, which could be put in the canteen.

Unit 8a: Global brands (Self-study)

Ex ❶:

1	cultural	2	advertising
3	globalise	4	adapts
5	production	6	universally
7	diverse	8	profitably

Ex ❷:

1	with	2	towards
3	with	4	to
5	round/around/on	6	as
7	from		

Ex ❸:

2	busy	hurried
3	essential	vital
4	domestic	national
5	cosmopolitan	diverse
6	robust	strong
7	classic	traditional
8	beneficial	advantageous

Ex ❹: **Suggested answer:** (140 words)

Report: Comparison of Serabi and Shanta Gold shares

At the start of the period Serabi and Shanta Gold share prices were both 33.5 pence. Yet, by the middle of February Serabi shares had reached 41 pence while Shanta Gold's had fallen slightly.

By mid-March both companies saw their share prices fall. Shanta Gold shares fell steeply from 33 pence to 28 pence, rising briefly before falling to a low of 26.5 pence. Prices picked up by the end of March and continued to show an overall upward trend finally reaching 32.5 pence in May, slightly lower than their price in early February.

Serabi's share price, however, following the sharp fall in March, picked up and increased steadily until mid-April by which time they had recovered to 38 pence. From then onwards there was a steady decrease in the price, reaching a low of 28.5 pence in early May.

Ex ❺: 2 spending power
3 target market
4 global presence
5 creative concept
6 marketing campaign

Ex ❻: 2 Rarely are our advertisements translated.
3 Never before has it been easier to advertise globally.
4 On no account should cultural differences be ignored.
5 Only in Europe have we had any success with it.
6 Under no circumstances should we change the logo.

Unit 8b: Global sourcing (Self-study)

Ex ❶: 1 B 2 C 3 B 4 A
5 B 6 C 7 B 8 B
9 A 10 C

Ex ❷: 1 No 2 No 3 No 4 Yes
5 Yes 6 No 7 Yes 8 No

Ex ❸: 2 warranty guarantee
3 attraction incentive
4 reputation image
5 plant machinery
6 premises buildings

Ex ❹: **Suggested answer:** (137 words)

Unemployment in Italy and Germany, 1993 to 1998

General trend
Unemployment figures in both Italy and Germany rose significantly over the period from 1993 to 1998.

Italy
Despite an overall increase, the unemployment figures were characterised by number of peaks and troughs over the six years. In 1993 unemployment stood at just over 9% of the total workforce, rising to 12% in 1995. It then fluctuated around this level until 1998, never falling below 11.5%.

Germany
In contrast, unemployment in Germany rose steadily with far fewer fluctuations, increasing from 8.5% to almost 10% by late 1993. Despite an improvement the following year, with the level falling to just under 9.25%, the

upward trend continued, with unemployment reaching a peak of 11.5% by the end of 1997. However, 1998 saw unemployment drop sharply to 10.7% before levelling off.

Ex ❺: 1 were confirmed
2 its
3 the
4 to win
5 who
6 had been holding out
7 had taken place
8 would have created
9 will not be releasing
10 are likely to
11 have also been circulating
12 announced
13 would be
14 are cutbacks feared
15 are made

Unit 8: Exam practice

L1: 1 networked computers 2 fear of criticism
3 creative energy 4 innovation
5 on merit 6 analysed objectively
7 no domination 8 secretary
9 drawings 10 distribution of documents
11 voting methods 12 favourite applications

L2: 13 E 14 C 15 G 16 D
17 H 18 J 19 L 20 P
21 O 22 M

L3: 23 B 24 B 25 C 26 B
27 C 28 A 29 A 30 B

R4: 1 C 2 D 3 B 4 C
5 A 6 A 7 D 8 C
9 D 10 B

Card list

		Number of cards
Unit 2a	Language of trends	6
Unit 3a	Jumbled letter	6
Exam focus: Speaking	Cards for Speaking Test Part One	12
Unit 6b	Role-cards for meeting (cultural values)	6
Unit 7a	Instructions for discussion (internal information)	6
Unit 8b	Role-cards for meeting (vested interests)	6

a dip

collapse

fluctuations

fallen

recovered

a high

Festival of Ceramics is always oversubscribed and by the time this letter reaches you, many of the available stands will already have been rebooked. Therefore, we recommend you reserve your stand as soon as possible and we guarantee all applications will be given our full attention the moment we receive them.

Pass Cambridge BEC Higher   Unit 3a 1/6

The key to the continuing popularity of the Festival of Ceramics is its selection of exhibitors, ensuring that buyers are seeing the very best in the industry. In addition the workshops, business seminars and show give additional support for people in the industry to make the right choices for them.

Pass Cambridge BEC Higher   Unit 3a 2/6

If you require any further information or advice, please do not hesitate to call Alex Whittle or myself on 0118 9784332 or email us on info@festivalofceramics.com

Pass Cambridge BEC Higher   Unit 3a 3/6

Now in its twenty-third year, Festival of Ceramics remains the largest UK-based exhibition for ceramics. From the smallest egg cups to the largest pots for the garden, all will be found. So, whatever your ceramic products there will be a place for them. The exhibition attracts has been attracting over 30,000 UK and overseas buyers since it moved to the NEC three years ago. Buyers who attend come from independent retailers, department stores, mail order houses and internet traders. If these are the people you need to meet, you will not be disappointed.

Pass Cambridge BEC Higher   Unit 3a 4/6

Thank you for your interest in the 2011 Festival of Ceramics show. As requested, I enclose full details of this and future shows for you.

Pass Cambridge BEC Higher   Unit 3a 5/6

Held in Birmingham the Festival of Ceramics attracts buyers who understand the importance of good design and practical products. The Festival allows you to meet customers, old and new, face to face, in an atmosphere that allows you to show your products to their best advantage.

Pass Cambridge BEC Higher   Unit 3a 6/6

your professional ambitions

Pass Cambridge BEC Higher   Exam focus: Speaking 1/12

your reasons for
learning English

Pass Cambridge BEC Higher   Exam focus: Speaking 2/12

what you like about your
job/studies

Pass Cambridge BEC Higher   Exam focus: Speaking 3/12

what you find difficult about
your job/studies

Pass Cambridge BEC Higher   Exam focus: Speaking 4/12

your interests outside work

Pass Cambridge BEC Higher   Exam focus: Speaking 5/12

your company

Pass Cambridge BEC Higher   Exam focus: Speaking 6/12

a place where you would
like to live

Pass Cambridge BEC Higher   Exam focus: Speaking 7/12

your dream job

Pass Cambridge BEC Higher   Exam focus: Speaking 8/12

something you are good at

Pass Cambridge BEC Higher   Exam focus: Speaking 9/12

your duties and
responsibilities

Pass Cambridge BEC Higher   Exam focus: Speaking 10/12

your qualifications
and experience

Pass Cambridge BEC Higher   Exam focus: Speaking 11/12

what you like about
where you live

Pass Cambridge BEC Higher   Exam focus: Speaking 12/12

Culture A

In your culture, team harmony is very important. Good qualifications and technical expertise are held to be essential and specialists who deliver high performance are often very well paid. Managers in your country are expected to speak English and often have international experience. Women often hold senior management positions and company structures are usually hierarchical. The style of management is usually authoritarian.

Culture B

In your culture, people believe in individual performance and recruiting the best specialist for any given position. Although the culture is very competitive and companies prefer to recruit young ambitious people, experience is often more important than qualifications. Management structures are often non-hierarchical and based on teams. There are also a lot of women in management.

Culture C

In your culture, harmony and stability are essential in the workplace. As people often work for one company all their lives, on the job training and experience are more important than qualifications. All pay negotiations are conducted collectively and any form of individual praise is embarrassing. Managers are almost always male and promoted from within the company. Their seniority is usually based on their length of service. Management structures are very hierarchical.

Culture D

You are from a culture which believes in consensus. People are usually recruited from within the company or the families of existing employees. Relationships with business partners are long-term and built on trust. Work routines are very standardised so very little decision-making is needed. Strategic decisions are made by senior managers, who are usually longserving and male. Pay is based on group and not individual performance.

Culture E

Your culture believes very strongly in social equality, so age and sex do not affect the recruitment process and companies recruit according to the specific requirements of the job. Management structures are usually flat but individual performance is encouraged and rewarded accordingly. Managers are good linguists and often have international experience. Qualifications are important, as is practical experience.

Culture F

Make proposals based on your own cultural values.

Agree and support the
speaker's argument

Pass Cambridge BEC Higher   Unit 7a 1/6

Disagree and state the
implications of the
speaker's idea

Pass Cambridge BEC Higher   Unit 7a 2/6

Give an opinion and justify it

Pass Cambridge BEC Higher   Unit 7a 3/6

Ask for someone's opinion

Pass Cambridge BEC Higher   Unit 7a 4/6

Give an opinion and clarify it

Pass Cambridge BEC Higher   Unit 7a 5/6

Ask the speaker to clarify
his/her point

Pass Cambridge BEC Higher   Unit 7a 6/6

Your vested interest

The owners of Consort Trading are very generous with their corporate hospitality and gift-giving. As the contact person, you would benefit from this most. Do your best to secure the contract for Consort Trading without anyone knowing why.

Your vested interest

You do not really like travelling and therefore do not want to do business with a distant company. Without giving the real reasons, try to persuade your colleagues to choose a central European supplier.

Your vested interest

The owners of The Namlong Sportswear Company have offered you a substantial personal financial reward if they manage to win the contract from your company. No-one else in your company knows about the offer.

Your vested interest

You are new to the company and have not travelled much on business before. Therefore, you are excited about the prospect of travelling to interesting, distant locations. Try to avoid your company choosing a central European supplier.

Your vested interest

Your brother is married to a Chinese woman. Members of her family own the Hai Xin Group and she put you in contact with the company. However, your colleagues do not know this. Your whole family would be very happy if Hai Xin won the contract. You would also be able to visit relatives while on business in China.

Your vested interest

Your company is experiencing financial difficulties and needs to cut costs wherever possible immediately. You have been made responsible for reducing the purchasing budget by as much as possible without making the company's financial position common knowledge.

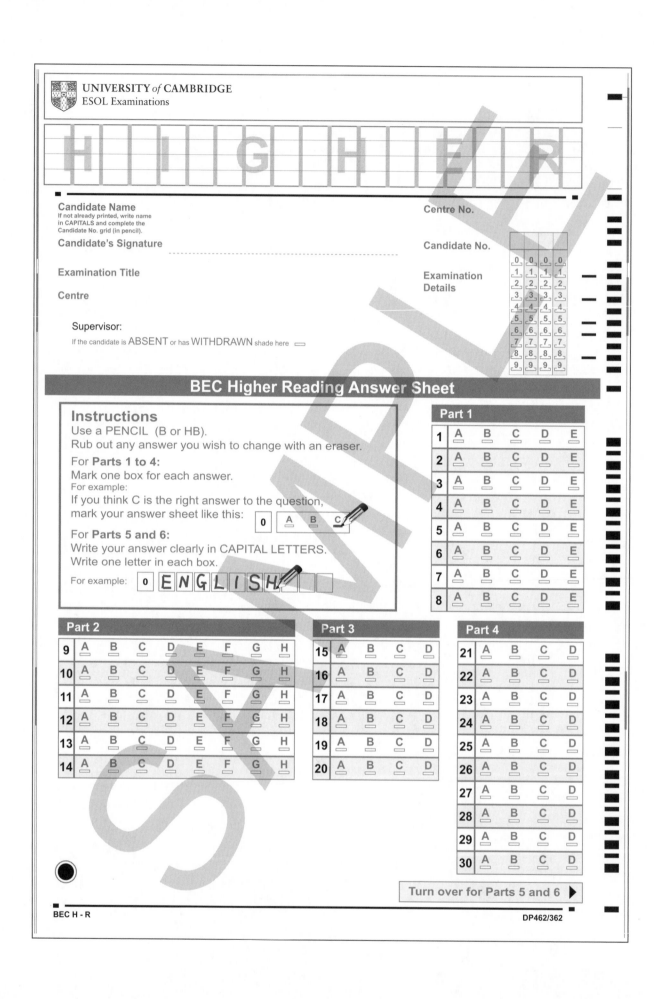

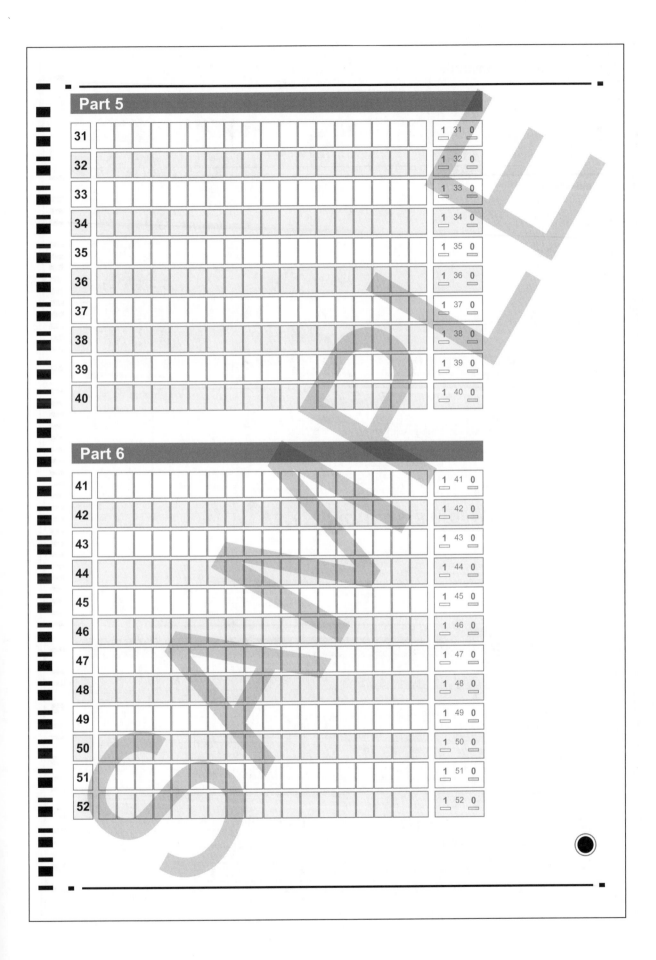

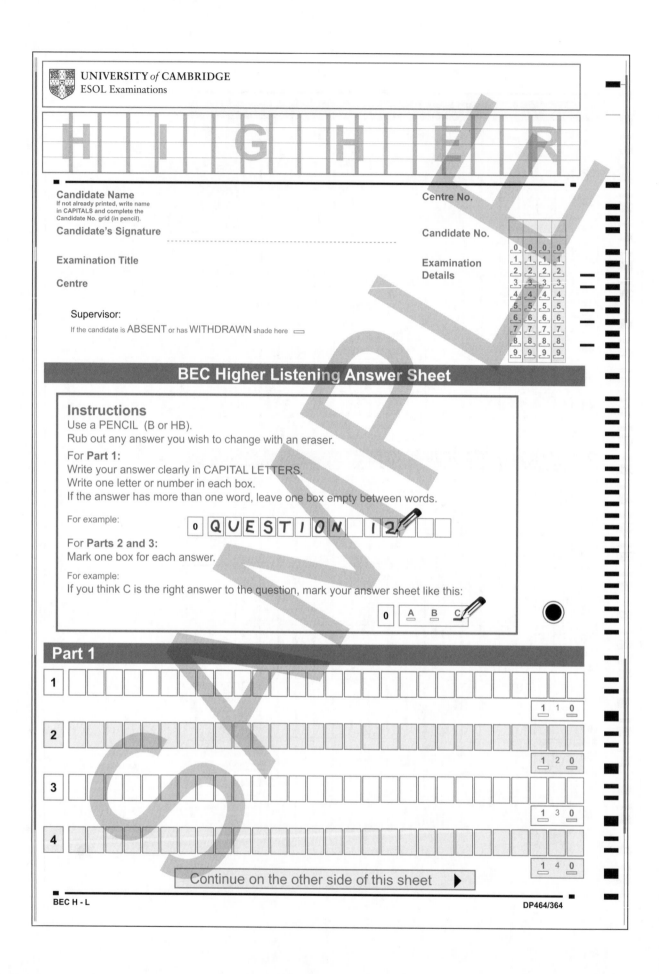

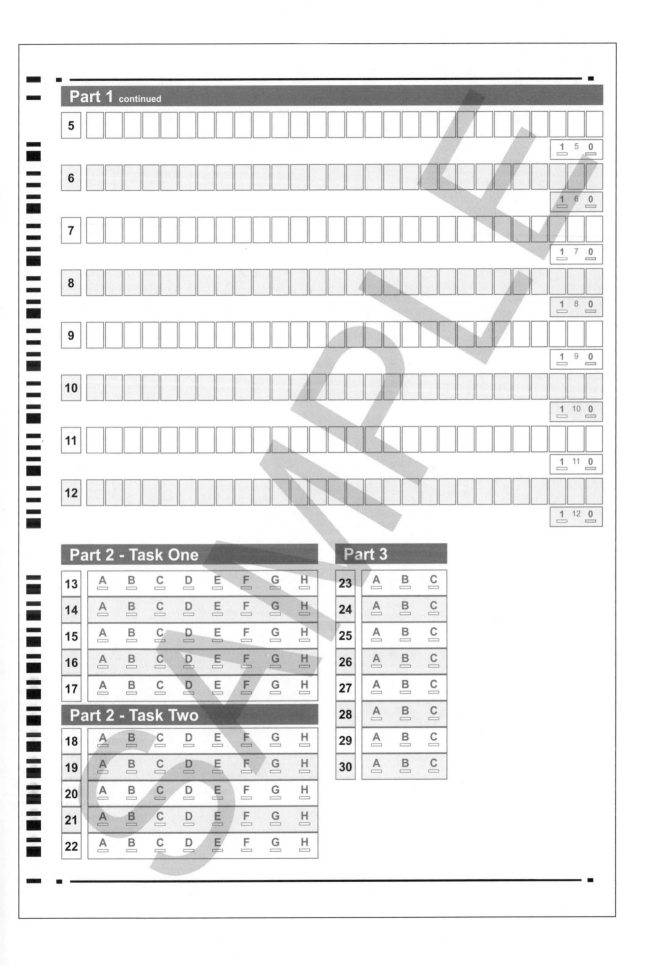

Part 1 continued

5   1 5 0

6   1 6 0

7   1 7 0

8   1 8 0

9   1 9 0

10   1 10 0

11   1 11 0

12   1 12 0

Part 2 - Task One

13	A	B	C	D	E	F	G	H
14	A	B	C	D	E	F	G	H
15	A	B	C	D	E	F	G	H
16	A	B	C	D	E	F	G	H
17	A	B	C	D	E	F	G	H

Part 2 - Task Two

18	A	B	C	D	E	F	G	H
19	A	B	C	D	E	F	G	H
20	A	B	C	D	E	F	G	H
21	A	B	C	D	E	F	G	H
22	A	B	C	D	E	F	G	H

Part 3

23	A	B	C
24	A	B	C
25	A	B	C
26	A	B	C
27	A	B	C
28	A	B	C
29	A	B	C
30	A	B	C